# FATHER, TEACHER, CHILD KILLER

## The Abduction of Louise Bell and Michael Black

### MICHAEL MADIGAN

Published in Australia by Elvis Press

First published in Australia 2025
This edition published 2025
Copyright © Michael Madigan 2025
Cover design, typesetting: WorkingType (www.workingtype.com.au)

The right of Michael Madigan to be identified as the
Author of the Work has been asserted in accordance with the
Copyright, Designs and Patents Act 1988.

All rights reserved. No part of this publication may be reproduced, stored in a retrieval system, or transmitted, in any form or by any means without the prior written permission of the publisher, nor be otherwise circulated in any form of binding or cover other than that in which it is published and without a similar condition being imposed on the subsequent purchaser.

ISBN: 978-1-7642602-0-6(PBK)

*For my beautiful granddaughter,*
*Rhiannon Mary Henry-Edwards*
*March 13, 2011 – October 8, 2023*

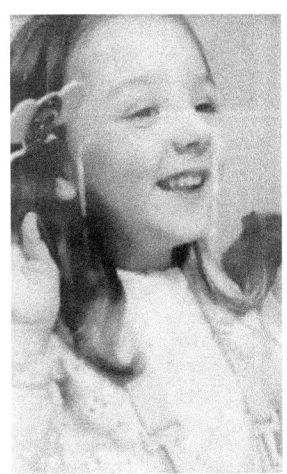

Rhiannon was an inspiration to everyone who knew her.

Though her life was short, her creativity knew no bounds.

She wrote stories that painted vivid worlds, a play that held us captivated for over an hour, and created art that reflected a soul far beyond her years.

She accomplished all this despite her disabilities, and with a spirit full of light, imagination, and courage.

We miss you so much, sweetheart.

# Contents

Prelude .................................................................. 1

## Part One: Louise Bell ............................................. 3

| Chapter 1 | January 3, 1983 ................................. 5 |
| Chapter 2 | The Morning After ........................ 14 |
| Chapter 3 | Ransom ............................................ 24 |
| Chapter 4 | February 6, 1983 ............................ 36 |
| Chapter 5 | Vital Clue ........................................ 45 |
| Chapter 6 | The Geesing Trial ......................... 54 |
| Chapter 7 | The Geesing Appeal ...................... 71 |
| Chapter 8 | "I am worried about Eloise..." ........ 77 |

## Part Two: Michael Black ..................................... 97

| Chapter 1 | 18 January 1989 ........................... 99 |
| Chapter 2 | The Morning after .................... 108 |
| Chapter 3 | The Reluctant Witness ............. 115 |
| Chapter 4 | The One That Got Away ......... 121 |
| Chapter 5 | Similar Facts ............................. 134 |
| Chapter 6 | Pfennig v Crown ....................... 137 |

| | | |
|---|---|---|
| **Part Three: Cold Case Review** | | **155** |
| Chapter 1 | Justice for Louise | 157 |
| Chapter 2 | Pfennig Back in Court | 162 |
| Chapter 3 | Prisoner Evidence | 189 |
| Chapter 4 | Deathbed Confession? | 201 |
| Chapter 5 | DNA | 203 |
| Chapter 6 | Judgement day | 214 |

And in the End... 218

## **Prelude**

Evil rarely announces itself.

It can take the form of a neighbour, a friendly shop assistant, or a man who waves as he passes on the street. We expect monsters to look like monsters—but they don't. They look like anyone.

Before tragedy strikes, there are often moments—subtle, fleeting—when something feels wrong. A disturbing remark. A stare that lingers too long. Small cruelties disguised as jokes. Too often, those who notice hesitate, unsure, unwilling to believe that darkness could be that close. But these warning signs matter. Sometimes, they are the only chance we have to stop what's coming.

In our modern world, technology stands guard. Cameras record our streets. GPS maps our movements. Messages can be traced, timelines reconstructed. These advances have made it harder for predators to vanish into anonymity.

Yet the same technology has a shadow side. It allows those with malicious intent to reach into our homes without ever crossing a threshold. Through a screen, they can befriend, deceive, and lure—targeting children from a distance, hidden behind layers of false names and stolen photographs. Safety and danger now travel on the same current.

This book tells the story of a murderer, but it is also about something larger—the uneasy truth that evil often hides in plain sight, that the very tools meant to protect us can be turned against us, and that one overlooked warning can change a life forever.

I have written these pages with respect and care for the families who have endured the most harrowing loss imaginable—the disappearance of a child. Their grief is not a chapter in a story; it is a lifetime without answers, without closure. I cannot pretend to understand the depth of their pain, but I can promise that this work was approached with the gravity and dignity such loss demands.

## PART ONE
# Louise Bell

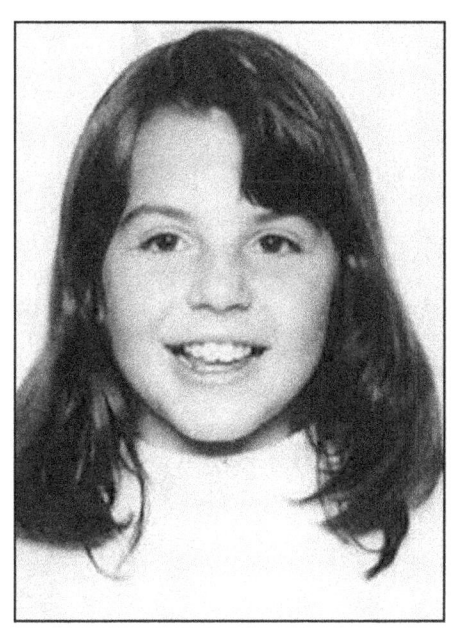

# Chapter 1

# January 3, 1983

It was a typical Adelaide summer day; the air was warm and dry, with the sky a flawless stretch of blue, devoid of a single cloud. Residents of the southern suburb of Hackham West eagerly anticipated the cool change predicted for later that night. As the sun melted into the horizon over St Vincent's Gulf, the temperature eased slightly. Still, within the cream-brick home of Colin (32) and Dianne Bell (32), the atmosphere remained uncomfortably warm, thick with the kind of stillness that felt both ordinary and, in hindsight, unsettling.

The doors and windows of their modest home were propped open, coaxing a reluctant southerly sea breeze to slip through. The excitement of Christmas had faded, but the school holidays were only halfway through. Louise (10) and Rachel (8), the Bell sisters, revelled in the freedom of school-free summer days. They were more than sisters; they were confidantes, partners in make-believe, their occasional squabbles dissolving as quickly as they flared.

At 7:30 pm, the girls were in their shared bedroom, a warm space filled with pop star posters, soft toys, and the fading twinkle of Christmas decorations. Their laughter drifted into the evening, mingling with the cicadas' song, marking the onset of nightfall.

The girls were excited about an upcoming trip to the cinema to see E.T., the blockbuster film directed by Steven Spielberg, a plan they had discussed with breathless anticipation, a level of excitement only children could muster. A family outing to the South Parklands in Adelaide's city centre was also planned for the following day. The Bell family were close-knit, their lives tightly woven together by shared routines and simple joys. Life felt secure and predictable. Wholesome.

Across the street, a neighbour glanced out her front window and paused, a soft smile tugging at the corners of her mouth. She had a clear view of the girls' brightly lit room. She watched as Louise and Rachel danced with carefree abandon, singing along to tunes from a cassette player—a treasured Christmas gift.

Later, after showers cooled their sun-kissed skin, the girls changed into light summer pyjamas. By 8:45 pm, the lights in the girls' bedroom were out, and the house gradually surrendered to darkness, save for the soft glow of a street lamp casting long, faint shadows across the front yard. At 10:00 pm, Colin and Dianne retired to their bedroom, only a thin wall away from their daughters. As was Colin's nightly ritual, he covered the pet budgie's cage in the kitchen, its soft rustling the last sound before quiet settled over the house. He then stepped onto the front porch, the screen door creaking briefly, to place empty milk bottles for the morning delivery.

Colin then went into the girls' room and lovingly kissed their foreheads.

"Sleep tight."

The neighbourhood seemed wrapped in tranquillity, but somewhere within that ordinary night, something unspoken stirred—an invisible thread unravelling, unnoticed until it was far too late.

## Part One   Chapter 1   January 3, 1983

At around 6 am, Dianne awoke to the sound of rattling glass bottles as the milkman delivered their daily supply to the front doorstep. She immediately got out of bed, went to the kitchen, and began her morning routine. After she put the kettle on, she walked down the carpeted passage to check on the girls.

She was confused by the sight of an empty bed; Louise was not there. She frantically checked every room in the house.

Confusion soon turned to anxiety as she rushed out the back door and called out for her daughter. "Louise... Louise!"

Dianne's movements quickened. She ran out the front door and jogged along the street. "Louise... Louise darling."

The street was deserted apart from a stray cat dashing down a drain.

Agitated, Dianne ran back inside her home and went to her bedroom, where she shook her sleeping husband. "Colin, Louise isn't in her room. I've looked everywhere."

Colin leapt out of bed. The parents entered the girls' bedroom and woke up eight-year-old Rachel.

"Rachel, where's Louise?"

Little Rachel rubbed her eyes and looked blankly back at her parents. She obviously had no idea where her big sister was.

Colin then noticed an opening in the wire screen window. The curtains were bunched together in the middle. He rushed across the road to 10 Meadow Way, which had a swimming pool in the backyard and searched there. He then ran to Louise's school, which was nearby on Glynville Drive. There was no one there.

After frantically searching the surrounding area, Colin returned home. He sat on the lounge chair to collect his thoughts. His stomach churned with fear, and his mind raced with panic. He reached for the phone and called the police to report the unthinkable: his daughter was missing.

Two police vehicles arrived within ten minutes. Young constables systematically knocked on doors in the neighbourhood. At the same time, two senior officers examined the girls' bedroom, which faced the street.

The small room was fitted with candy-striped curtains from floor to ceiling, with both bedheads positioned below the window ledge. The bedroom was a typical one for young girls. Pop idol posters were sticky-taped to the walls, toys crowded the cupboards, and a basketball trophy stood proud and prominent on the dressing table.

Louise loved playing basketball for the local Saints team and had been presented with the trophy only a month earlier.

Police quickly noticed that the window's wire screen had been tampered with. The screen, made of synthetic mesh material, had an opening that appeared large enough for a small child to squeeze through. Aside from the screen, there were no other signs of disturbance. Within 30 minutes, two detectives from the Christies Beach Police Station arrived and began questioning the parents.

Colin and Dianne sat close together on one side of the round timber kitchen table. The two detectives were seated directly opposite them. The senior detective spoke in a soft yet assertive tone as he questioned the parents, who were both trembling in a state of shock.

Colin Bell told police that when he said goodnight to his girls, he remembered seeing the sliding window in the girls' room was only

## Part One  Chapter 1  January 3, 1983

slightly open on one side and that the curtains had fully covered the window. In the morning, he found the curtains pushed to one side with the sliding window fully extended. Bell informed police that the flyscreen on the girls' window had minor damage before that evening. Still, he believed the damage was now far more extensive.

Police pressed the Bells for any information.

"No, we don't know of any reason why she would run away."

"She was happy, a shy girl, and quiet... she would never run away from home."

"There is no reason in the world for her to leave home."

"No, I haven't seen any stranger lurking around..."

Louise was described as being around 4 feet 6 inches (135 cm) tall, with short brown hair, tanned skin, and dark brown eyes. Dianne Bell told the detectives that Louise wore bright orange shortie pyjamas when she tucked her daughter in and kissed her goodnight.

Dianne's voice rose. "She's asthmatic; she needs her puffer." She put her head in her hands and started weeping.

The neighbours of the Bell family spilled out onto the street, huddling in tight groups, their hushed voices barely masking their shock. The sheer enormity of the situation unfolding before them cast a heavy pall over the neighbourhood. In Hackham West, a suburb already scarred by tragedy, the chilling thought that yet another child had vanished sent ripples of dread through the community.

Kirste Gordon had lived only a few hundred metres from the Bell home. She was only four years old when she and eleven-year-old Joanne Ratcliffe were abducted from Adelaide Oval in August 1973, snatched in broad daylight during a football match attended by over

12,000 people. Neither girl was ever seen again.

Now, with the disappearance of yet another girl from the same area, the eerie coincidence sparked a wave of speculation that spread like wildfire. Whispers turned into accusations. Men who had lived quietly in the district for years were subjects of dark suspicion. Paranoia festered behind drawn curtains.

Within hours, one of the most extensive searches in South Australian police history occurred. The thumping sound of the State Rescue helicopter made broad sweeps of the district and then headed along the pristine coastal beaches nearby. The State Emergency Service and over one hundred Country Fire Service personnel scoured the area, checking the dry creeks and the nearby bushland.

The Bell home was typical of houses built in the early 1970s, featuring cream brick and a green tiled roof with three bedrooms.

Hackham West is a working-class suburb situated between the Onkaparinga Hills to the east and the Onkaparinga River, as well as the southern beaches to the west. Approximately 25 kilometres from Adelaide's CBD, it was not your typical capital city suburb. Among the numerous symmetrical rows of houses were thick tracts of bushland, a nearby conservation park with its rugged terrain and dozens of deep, secluded gullies.

Eight-year-old Rachel Bell looked apprehensive as she climbed into the back of the powder blue Holden Commodore police car. She waved to her mother as she was driven down Meadow Way onto Glynville Drive. Detectives hoped the shaken but brave little girl could show them where her big sister used to play and visit.

Police urgently sent descriptions and photographs of Louise to police stations across the state. It was obvious that South Australian Police chiefs were working on a well-organised plan. It had been ten years since the Ratcliffe and Gordon abduction. South Australian Police now had the help of a newly installed computer system to organise the vast amount of information that they would soon be gathering.

A police command post was established in a cramped caravan at Hackham West Primary, only 100 metres from the Bell family home. The air was thick with uncertainty as officers, still on edge, hesitated to label Louise's disappearance as an abduction. They were considering three possible scenarios, each more chilling than the last.

**The first:** Louise had left home on her own. But why? What could have driven a child to vanish without a trace?

**The second:** She left willingly but was taken afterwards.

**The third** — and the most terrifying — was abduction. Police were sure she had either crawled or been dragged through the window; the damaged screen pushed outward as if from inside the room. Clearly, the flyscreen had been tampered with, but was it a deliberate decoy designed to mislead them and send them down the wrong trail?

Questions lingered, each one more pressing than the last. Had the abductor entered through the front or back door, and how had they managed to carry Louise away undetected? Was the Bell home truly secure, or had someone been in the house before? How could a child disappear in the dead of night without a single sound breaking the silence? The more the police dug, the more the mystery deepened — and the more the fear settled in.

Colin Bell had spent the entire day pacing the streets and searching the parks around Hackham West, his heart heavy with a fear that grew stronger with every hour. Friends and family walked with him, their steps quiet, eyes scanning for any sign of Louise—anything that might bring them closer to her.

Colin's legs felt like lead as the sun began to set, weighed down by exhaustion and the crushing dread that tightened with each unanswered question. When he finally turned onto his street, the sight that greeted him made his heart thud—police cars lined the road, their flashing lights vivid and unmistakable even in the fading light. As he approached the front door, he silently prayed that Louise would be inside, sitting on her mother's lap, smiling. But Louise wasn't there.

Instead, the living room was filled with stern-faced men in dark suits, their expressions cold and unreadable; their presence serving as a grim reminder of the situation.

His wife sat on the sofa, her face pale and hollow, her eyes empty with fear and exhaustion, broken by an ordeal no parent should ever face. Her hands gripped a tissue, twisted and crumpled beyond recognition, mirroring the fragile hope with which they had started the day.

Down the narrow hallway, men clad head to toe in white forensic suits moved meticulously, their gloved hands methodically dusting, lifting, and searching. They hovered in Louise's bedroom—a space once filled with the innocent chaos of a child's life, now a sterile, silent crime scene. Teddy bears and school books stood witness as strangers sifted through her belongings, hoping to find a clue, a fragment of evidence that might explain the unthinkable.

By nightfall, the words no family ever wants to hear were spoken aloud: Louise Bell's disappearance was now officially declared a major crime.

And somewhere in the darkness, the answers for which Colin Bell prayed were already slipping further out of reach.

## Chapter 2

# The Morning After

The first night without Louise was torment. For Colin and Dianne Bell, sleep offered no escape, only a deeper descent into the nightmare. Colin, fuelled by desperate hope, had spent hours with police scouring the neighbourhood, the silence of the streets amplifying his growing dread. Returning to his wife's side, he collapsed onto the lounge.

Oblivious to the terror gripping her parents, little Rachel slept on, a stark contrast to the chaos unfolding around her.

Morning brought the harsh glare of the media pack. Twenty-plus reporters and photographers crowded the Bells' small lounge room. Colin's voice trembled as he spoke. "It's like a bad dream," he managed. It was the cliché, a stark truth in this context. "We love Louise very much and want her to come home. It doesn't matter if she's done anything wrong." His words were a plea, a fragile shield against the unthinkable. "Just some knowledge that she's all right would be a relief. We are worried that she may have an asthma attack if she is in trouble. We're worried sick about her, but I still think she is all right. We believe she will come home to us sometime today." Hope was a flickering candle in the encroaching darkness. Colin described his daughter as a "pretty little girl with a nice smile." He then revealed a chilling detail. During his frantic search, he'd had... "a feeling she was close by. Still, by morning, I had lost that gut feeling." Colin's voice trembled as he spoke.

The question of Louise's possible voluntary departure hung heavy in the air.

"It is bizarre," Colin admitted, the word inadequate to capture the surreal horror of the situation. "Sometimes you have to think about things that are bizarre." He wrestled with the possibilities, each one a fresh wave of agony. "Louise either went of her own accord or was enticed. I just don't know."

*Colin and Dianne Bell with daughter Rachel.*

The tearful father's appeal was heart-wrenching: "I want people to look at their children and try to think what they would do." This is a universal plea, tapping into the primal fear that every parent shares. "People could look in their backyards, sheds, empty houses, or even holiday shacks."

The cold, hard facts offered little comfort. A meticulous

examination by police technical services officers yielded nothing: no forced entry, no struggle, no trace of her abductor. Not even an unknown fingerprint was found.

"We have searched all her favourite haunts, people have been questioned, and everything from drains to bins checked," Superintendent Lenton told the assembled media, his words laced with grim reality. "Obviously, the fact that we have been unable to turn up anything new is worrying."

Worrying. An understatement that echoed the growing fear in everyone's hearts.

The police launched a massive publicity campaign, plastering Louise's image on posters, buses, and newspapers. They knew time was running out. Every passing hour diminished the chances of finding her alive. Information booths popped up in shopping centres, desperate for a lead, a whisper, anything. A family friend provided a video of Louise and her friends, a precious glimpse of her life before it vanished, now used by television stations — a constant reminder of the missing girl, a face etched into the public consciousness.

Louise was filmed laughing and playing at a pool party during the end-of-season basketball presentation in November 1982.

In the days following Louise Bell's disappearance, Hackham West—a suburb once alive with the carefree laughter of children—fell into an eerie, suffocating silence. This was a neighbourhood built for young families, where bikes usually lay sprawled on front lawns, and the rhythmic thud of basketballs and footballs echoed down quiet streets. But now, the only sounds were the occasional bark of a restless dog and the faint hum of television sets behind locked doors.

The parks, once dotted with picnics and playground games, stood deserted. Swings creaked idly in the breeze, their empty seats swaying like fragile reminders of what had been stolen—not only Louise but a sense of safety, a fragile illusion shattered overnight. Sleepovers, once a routine part of childhood, were no longer considered. Doors were bolted, and windows nailed shut. Children clung to their parents at bedtime, terrified not only of the dark but of what—or who—might be lurking beyond it.

Men who had once spent weekends tending to gardens were now reinforcing screen doors and replacing locks. Locksmith vans became as common a sight as postmen, their presence a quiet acknowledgment of a neighbourhood gripped by fear. Parents weren't just concerned; they were terrified.

As the days passed without answers, the community's grief turned to frustration. Residents gathered, signing a petition demanding that streetlights remain on through the night as if a wash of artificial light could keep the darkness—and the danger—at bay. Their voices were heard. Police patrols became a constant, their presence a double-edged sword: both a comfort and a reminder that something unthinkable had happened right here, on streets they'd once thought safe.

Five long days passed—five days without a trace of Louise, without a shred of a hopeful lead. Then, a press conference was called. The media descended, their cameras poised, microphones lined up like soldiers. But when Colin and Dianne Bell stepped forward, even the most seasoned reporters fell silent.

The transformation was staggering. Within days, the couple's faces had been etched with lines of grief and exhaustion, their once-vibrant expressions hollowed by worry. Colin's shoulders sagged under an invisible weight; his eyes clouded with a pain no words could fully convey. Dianne stood beside him, her face gaunt, lips pressed into a thin line, her hands clenched tightly—as if holding on to hope itself. Yet when they spoke, their voices didn't tremble. "We hope every day that she is coming home," Colin said, his words cutting through the heavy silence like a blade. "We will never lose hope that she is coming home to us—that she is somewhere."

It was the kind of hope that could break hearts; the type that clung to life even when everything else seemed lost. And as the cameras clicked and reporters scribbled notes, no one in that room could deny the simple, searing truth: hope can be both the light that guides you and the pain that tears you apart.

Detective Gerry Edwards began by stating that, although there was no hard evidence to support the theory of an abduction, it was a matter of reality. "If she left of her own accord, why haven't we seen or heard from her?" He then confirmed that S.A. Police had called for files from a similar abduction in Melbourne in 1976. He noted that the disappearance of Louise closely resembled that of Eloise Worledge (8), who was abducted from her bedroom in Melbourne's suburb of Beaumaris. The anniversary of Eloise's disappearance was the following day. She had also disappeared after a flyscreen on the window of her room had been cut open. Eloise had not been seen since.

Colin Bell revealed that he and his wife had barely slept since the disappearance and had spent hours with detectives over the weekend going through school reports, old photographs—"Anything which might give some clue."

Asked about the likelihood of Louise's being enticed from the house, Dianne Bell said, "She has been warned constantly about strangers. She is just not the type to do that sort of thing."

Colin Bell stated that neither he, his wife, nor their younger daughter, Rachel, had heard anything during the night.

The experienced journalists, as well as the young cadets, looked spellbound by the mystery and misery unfolding before them. The strain of discussing their lost child began to take its toll. Both parents started to shed tears, their lips quivering.

After a minute to compose himself, Colin Bell said, "Our faith is that she is alive. We only pray that someone has not forced... I don't think anyone could have... just look at her face." He continued, "And to anyone who might have her, even if they just leave her in a phone box a hundred miles from here, please do... leave her where we can find her." His voice began breaking mid-sentence, prompting the police media officer to call the conference to a close. Colin bowed his head as tears flowed once again. A doctor embraced Dianne Bell and escorted her to a room where she was sedated.

**Mystics and Millionaires**

When millionaire Adelaide real estate tycoon Con Polites announced that he was offering a $5,000 reward for information regarding the disappearance of Louise, it was clear this tragedy was following the well-worn path of previous child abductions in Adelaide. Polites was also proactive in the search for the three missing Beaumont children back in 1966. He contributed to bringing world-renowned Dutch psychic Gerard Croiset to Australia to solve the Beaumont children's mystery. This would prove to be Croiset's most public failure, but would also contribute to the rising popularity of the psychic detective.

Croiset claimed that the siblings were buried under a specific warehouse. A thorough search of the building in November 1966 yielded nothing, as did another excavation in the 1990s funded by Polites.

The millionaire described the government's $5,000 reward as "a pittance these days." "When I saw Mr Bell's face in The News yesterday, I was moved by his despair."

Of course, the mystics didn't take long to seek publicity from this tragedy.

Doris Stokes, the English clairvoyant who had given false hope to the Beaumont, Ratcliffe, and Gordon families, was interviewed from London by Jeremy Cordeaux of radio station 5DN.

She described Meadow Way, the street where Louise Bell lived, and the "open fields" at the end of it. During the interview, Stokes stated that she believed the girl was still alive. She said there had been no struggle when Louise left her home.

As she was speaking, Stokes said she felt a prick on the arm, "as though somebody put a needle in it." She said "they" were very good at their job so as not to wake the other child, her sister Rachel, who was asleep in the same bedroom. As Stokes spoke of the fields at the end of Meadow Way, she said she saw a large white car, not a station wagon, with three people: two men and a woman.

Then she felt the car was heading up a winding road to "lofty."

"Before I get to the top, somewhere there is some water, still water."

Stokes speculated that Louise had been taken from her room around 2 am.

## January 13, 1983

It was nearing 11 pm, and the Bell household was cloaked in a fragile, uneasy stillness. Colin and Dianne lay on their bed, fully clothed, their arms instinctively wrapped around their younger daughter, Rachel, who had nestled between them. The little girl had finally drifted into a restless sleep, but sleep was a distant luxury for her parents—an indulgence they couldn't afford. Their minds kept repeating the same unbearable questions: Where is she? Who took her? Is she scared? Is she...? The weight of the silence was crushing, filled only by the occasional rustle of the sheets as Colin shifted or Dianne's quiet, stifled sobs. Then, without warning, the shrill ring of the house phone cut through the stillness, its sound sharp and jarring—a sound that hadn't meant much only days ago, but now carried the potential to either deliver peace or shatter their last thread of hope.

Colin bolted upright, his heart pounding violently. He sprinted to the lounge room, his bare feet slapping against the cool floorboards. For a fragile second, he allowed himself to believe—this is it, the police have news, maybe even... He snatched the receiver, his voice breathless, trembling with the desperation he tried to contain.

"Colin speaking." A pause. Just long enough to raise every hair on the back of his neck.

Then came a voice. It wasn't familiar or comforting. It was cold, flat, and devoid of emotion. "Colin Bell?"

"Yes... Who's this?" His grip tightened on the phone; his knuckles white.

"I have your daughter. I want thirty thousand dollars, or she will be killed."

The sentence hung in the air, thick and suffocating. Colin's breath caught in his chest. His knees buckled slightly, but he didn't fall. He couldn't.

"What—what did you say?" he managed to stammer.

Colin Bell felt sick to the stomach; he was so stunned he couldn't find a suitable reply to the would-be kidnapper.

"If you don't do as I say, bang, she is dead."

The caller told Bell he would call around midday the next day and warned him not to contact the police.

"Do as I say, and you can speak to Louise for five minutes."

The phone went dead.

Colin stood, the receiver still pressed to his ear, the dial tone buzzing into the silence. His mind raced, trying to reconcile what he'd just heard. Hope and terror collided inside him.

He stumbled back into the bedroom and turned on the light. Dianne sat up instantly, her instincts screaming before he even spoke.

"What is it? Colin—what's wrong? Who rang?"

His dry mouth opened, but for a second, no words came out. Then, in barely a whisper, he said, "Someone said they have Louise. They want money..."

Dianne's face crumpled, her hands flying to her mouth as if to physically contain the scream rising in her throat.

Colin's demeanour of helplessness turned to outrage and anger; a raw, burning fury at the cruel voice on the other end of the line.

Whether it was true or not, someone knew that saying those words would break them.

And it did.

But it also steeled them. Because now they had something—anything—to hold onto. Even if it was only a voice in the dark.

## Chapter 3

# Ransom

The minutes after the call felt like hours. Colin Bell sat frozen, knowing he had to inform the police, but also haunted by the previous caller's warning about what would happen to Louise if he contacted them.

The sound of the phone ringing startled him.

He snatched the receiver, bracing himself for the cold, emotionless voice that had tormented him since the last call.

"Hello? Colin speaking."

But it wasn't the same voice. "Colin, it's Detective Sergeant Harris from Major Crime." The voice was steady and authoritative—like a lifeline tossed into dark, turbulent waters. "Listen carefully. We've fitted your phone with a trace device. If he calls again, we'll track him. Stay calm, Colin. We're on our way."

The words should've been comforting, but only added to the tangled knot of fear.

Colin hung up, his hand trembling as he shared the news with Dianne. The relief was fleeting. Hope felt dangerous and fragile now.

Within the hour, their quiet home, once filled with the laughter of two little girls, had become a staging ground for law enforcement. Detectives from Major Crime arrived, their faces revealing both empathy and steely determination. They spread out efficiently, notebooks open.

The Bells' phone was fitted with a simple voice recorder attached to a cassette player. The detectives played and replayed the telephone conversation numerous times to catch any clues about who the offender could be.

Colin and Dianne sat huddled on the worn couch, with Rachel asleep in their bedroom under the watchful eye of a female officer. The soft hum of police radios, the scratch of pens on paper, and the occasional whisper all felt surreal, as if they were actors in someone else's nightmare. But this was their reality.

Each minute felt like an hour. Then, minutes after midnight, the breakthrough came. Telephone technicians had established a trace. The signal led them to Lutana Crescent in Mitchell Park—a quiet street where porch lights flickered, and the world seemed oblivious to the darkness that had settled over one family.

At 3 am, police surrounded a modest weatherboard house. The stillness was shattered with a sharp knock on the door. "Police, open up."

There was no answer. Then, movement—a light flicked on, and the door creaked open. A young woman, dishevelled and bleary-eyed, squinted against the glare of police torches.

Officers surged past her before she could form a question, sweeping through the house with clinical precision. Every room was searched—closets flung open, beds lifted, drawers yanked out. They weren't only looking for evidence; they were searching for a child.

But Louise wasn't there.

Instead, on a cluttered coffee table near the phone, officers found a newspaper. The headline screamed Louise's name, and the article had been crudely highlighted in thick black marker, the ink pressing so hard it almost tore through the page.

The male occupant of the house—a wiry, twitchy twenty-year-old named Gregory Paul Durdin—watched the search with a thin veneer of defiance that didn't quite mask his underlying fear. Durdin wasn't a stranger to the law. A petty criminal with a record of minor offences, he carried himself with the bravado of someone who'd spent time behind locked doors.

Under the stark fluorescent lights at the police station, his story shifted like sand in the wind. First, he denied the call. Then he blamed an unnamed friend. Eventually, he claimed it was a fellow inmate from his days at McNalley Training Centre, a juvenile facility notorious for housing boys who'd already flirted with the edges of the law.

But Durdin's lies unravelled quickly. The evidence—the phone trace, the newspaper, his evasive answers—painted a damning picture.

In court, his demeanour was a mix of arrogance and indifference. He pled not guilty, as if the words themselves could erase the horror he'd inflicted on a family already drowning in grief. But the judge saw through him. The sentencing was swift: five years imprisonment for extortion, a crime made even more grotesque by its context.

Yet, even as the courtroom doors closed behind him, there was no sense of victory. No relief. Because Gregory Paul Durdin had nothing to do with Louise's disappearance, he was just another shadow in the dark—a parasite feeding off someone else's tragedy.

For Colin and Dianne, the nightmare continued. The unanswered questions lingered. The empty bed remained.

And somewhere, out there, was the truth. Still waiting to be found.

## January 17, 1983

Police revealed that they had interviewed a man whom they classified as a person of interest in Louise's abduction. The man had recently been arrested for multiple sexual crimes against a 14-year-old girl and was on bail awaiting trial for these offences. He also had been living close to the Bells' home for several years before the abduction. Police thoroughly searched his home and took away several items, including a pair of sneakers.

Later that evening, the case took a bizarre twist.

At 9:10 pm, Ms S, a neighbour of the Bell family, was winding down from her day, the soft glow of the television casting flickering shadows across her living room. The sharp ring of the telephone shattered the tranquillity. On the other end, a male voice—quavering, marked by a slight European accent—introduced himself with chilling urgency: he was Louise Bell's abductor.

Ms S later recounted to police the unnerving panic in the caller's voice. "I need your help; it's a desperate situation. I'm worried about Eloise... I mean, Louise," he stammered. His frantic plea for medical advice sent a jolt of fear through her. Alarmed, she scrambled to find a pen and paper, her hands shaking as she took meticulous notes.

The caller's desperation was palpable. "Your help could save Louise's life," he insisted.

Ms S urged him to contact the authorities, suggesting he ring a hospital. His response was equally disturbing: "I can't call any place where my voice could be traced." He rambled incoherently about "tones and frequencies," his words tangled in a web of paranoia.

Between strained breaths, the man claimed Louise was "with them," that she was "happy and did not want to go home." His insistence grew more unsettling as he pressed Ms S for medical guidance. When she mentioned Louise's asthma, he quickly dismissed it. "Her asthma is under control," he replied, as if he knew intimately.

He provided two phone numbers: one for The News and the other for Channel Nine television. He was eager for exposure. Then, his tone shifted, describing Louise's injuries with clinical detachment, the nature of which made Ms S's stomach churn. Her hand trembled as she jotted down each horrific detail, her mind reeling from the gruesome implications.

Ms S, gathering her courage, questioned the authenticity of the call. The man responded with chilling specificity: "Her earrings can be found if the police look under a brick at the corner of South Road and Beach Road."

His contempt for the authorities was evident. He mocked the South Australian Police, calling them "stupid," and claimed they had "missed a number of things." He elaborated on the crime scene, noting that any girl running away wouldn't escape through a noisy window. He mentioned the flywire screen had been "eased out and stretched, not pushed from the inside."

Ms S, recalling her walks past the Bell home, remembered the damaged screen predated the abduction. She challenged the caller, who confirmed, "Yes, it was already broken."

He added another eerie detail: tent wires beneath the window had been moved to avoid noise. When Ms S asked why he had called her specifically, he claimed her number was chosen randomly from the phone book.

Determined to end the disturbing exchange, Ms S informed him she would contact the police. She hung up and immediately did so.

Police acted swiftly. A patrol car raced to the intersection of Beach Road and Main South Road in Hackham West. Under the beam of a flashlight, an officer spotted a broken brick on the footpath. Carefully overturning it, he revealed a pair of delicate gold earrings, their shine stark against the dark soil. The officer placed them in a paper bag and rushed to the Bell residence.

Colin Bell cradled the earrings in his palm, his gaze fixed on them for over a minute. Finally, he nodded solemnly. "They're Louise's." He recognised a distinct mark, the handiwork of Louise's grandfather, who had once repaired them.

The case had veered into a surreal nightmare. The earrings were a double-edged sword for the Bells—a fragment of hope that Louise might still be alive, yet a terrifying clue pointing to the depravity of her abductor. The caller's cryptic claim that Louise was "with them" haunted Louise's parents and the investigators. Was it a sinister smokescreen to obscure his identity, or did it hint at a more complex web of perpetrators? The questions mounted, each more chilling than the last.

## "Louise in the Adelaide area"

Police held a press conference the following morning and announced that there had been a significant breakthrough in the investigation into the abduction. Police revealed that they believed Louise Bell was being held in the Adelaide area and that she needed urgent medical treatment. Police kept the fact that Ms S had received a

*The location where Louise Bell's earrings were found*

phone call secret. Reporters pounced on the report with follow-up questions, but police naturally declined to disclose any specifics. When one journalist asked about previous abductions in Adelaide, Senior Sergeant Edwards responded by admitting that Adelaide had a "bizarre reputation" for child abductions but said there are dangers in drawing comparisons between the disappearance of Louise Bell and the three Beaumont children from Glenelg and Joanne Ratcliffe and Kirste Gordon from Adelaide Oval. "These children were taken in broad daylight from public places, whereas Louise Bell was taken from her home in darkness".

Mr Bell looked more buoyant as he faced the media. He said the medical problem was not his daughter's asthmatic condition. He said he and his wife were aware of "a couple of things" it could be, but he did not want to speculate further.

Colin Bell made an impassioned plea for information regarding Louise's whereabouts.

"Whoever has Louise, let her go."

"Just leave her in a safe place where she can be found".

"Leave her at a telephone box, shop, or anywhere safe. We are not interested in you."

"You can disappear into the night – but let her go."

Colin Bell said the latest development had started his family's anguish "all over again."

He asked for his daughter to be left somewhere safe and for "them" to call someone responsible and let them know where she is. "They can call the ambulance or the press if they want to."

## Back to School

The first week of February carried a quiet grief through Hackham West, which settled over the streets like an unwelcome shadow. Louise Bell's absence was a hollow space in the hearts of her family and the community, an ache that words struggled to fill.

On the first day of the school year, Rachel Bell clutched her parents' hands tightly as they walked her to school. Her small fingers intertwined with Colin and Dianne's, a fragile tether to normalcy amid their unravelling world. At the classroom door, Rachel broke free, rushing to join her friends with the eager innocence only a child could still muster. But for Colin and Dianne, even briefly, the act of letting go felt like losing another piece of their heart.

Other parents approached with gentle words and sympathetic glances, their voices soft, weighed down by an unspoken fear—the fear that it could have been their child. Dianne offered polite thanks, her voice steady despite the turmoil inside her. Colin could only nod, his head lowered, as if the weight of grief was too much to bear. His tears were held back, like a dam on the verge of bursting.

Outside the school gates, the media waited—ever vigilant, ever hungry. A journalist's question pierced the fragile quiet. Asking Colin Bell how he was coping.

Colin's response was measured, yet raw: "It has been the hardest day for my family since Louise disappeared. Seeing other children walk past our home on their way to school was greatly upsetting." His voice faltered slightly, but he stood firm in his belief, echoing a hope that refused to die. "We have had no news to the contrary. We still believe our daughter is alive."

Colin and Dianne walked home hand-in-hand, their figures cast in long morning shadows, a picture of love mixed with deep pain.

*Colin and Dianne Bell*

At Hackham West Primary, hundreds of children gathered for assembly. The headmaster, Mr M Horsnell, stood before them, his voice a fragile thread in the morning air. "As many of you will have heard, Louise is not with us today. We are trying very hard to find her, to have her back at Hackham West Primary with us, and to bring her home to her parents."

In Louise's classroom, her empty chair sat like an open wound.

The media captured the haunting image—a small desk, untouched, surrounded by the bustling life of children who could not fully grasp the depth of the tragedy. Members of the Major Crime Squad arrived later, their serious faces in stark contrast to the colourful walls adorned with children's artwork. They spoke gently to the students, asking them to remember and think hard, hoping that a small detail might hold the key to finding Louise.

But it wasn't only the Bell family drowning in sorrow. Louise's grandparents, Marie and Norm Gibbs, bore their heavy grief.

"The wait for us is like a cancer... the agony is endless. It is with us every day... it has broken our hearts," Marie confessed, her voice cracking under the weight of despair.

They pleaded through the media, their words a desperate prayer: "She is still alive," Marie insisted, clinging to hope with the ferocity of a grandmother's love. "Every morning, I get up and walk to the front door to see if Louise is there on our front lawn. I have this feeling that one morning she is going to be there, waiting for us."

Sleep was a luxury they no longer knew. Their nights were filled with restless drives to the Bell home, searching for answers in the dark. "She was Nana's girl and would always confide in me," Marie whispered, her voice thick with longing. "Why won't he tell us where she is?"

When the pain became too much, even the smallest reminder could unravel them. A shopping trip to Target, a missing poster with Louise's smiling face—each glimpse was a fresh wound. "She must have been taken... But she is still alive. She was a beautiful girl—she still is."

Marie believed the police had good leads. Her intuition painted a picture of the abductor: "A young man, in his 30s, very lonely and frustrated. He could have watched her for a long time. He must have known she slept in that bedroom and knew when to take her. But why was it Louise and why this house?"

Her questions hung in the air, heavy and unanswered. The only certainty was Louise's echoing absence, a void that refused to be filled.

## Chapter 4

# February 6, 1983

Detective John Woite of Major Crime wasn't one to overlook details. When he stepped into the role of Administration Sergeant in the investigation of Louise's disappearance, he carried with him a reputation for precision and an unflinching commitment to procedure. A tall, well-built man, Woite was in charge of a team of seven major crime detectives, including Detective Paul Madden and Detective Lyn Strange as the primary detectives.

Upon reviewing the case files, Woite felt a growing unease. The initial door-to-door canvassing efforts, critical in the early days of any missing persons case, seemed scattershot—a patchwork of missed opportunities and inconsistent follow-ups. It was clear to him: the neighbourhood had spoken, but not everyone had been truly heard.

Determined to rectify this, Woite issued a directive that was as methodical as it was relentless. Every residence in Hackham West and its surrounding areas would be revisited. If no one answered a knock, that absence would be meticulously documented, and officers would return until contact was made. No door would remain unanswered. Alongside this renewed canvassing effort, Woite crafted a series of fifteen pointed questions designed not just to gather facts, but to unearth the overlooked, the seemingly insignificant details that might, in retrospect, hold the key to Louise's fate. Any response that hinted at inconsistency, anomaly, or suspicion would be flagged for immediate follow-up.

Yet, Woite wasn't content with relying solely on interviews. He needed to visualise the crime, to breathe life into the sterile facts of reports and statements. He organised a re-enactment at the Bell home—a sombre exercise where young officers, chosen for their varying statures, attempted to replicate potential abduction scenarios. They detached the flyscreen just as it had been found, reaching through the window into the small, innocent space Louise had shared with her sister, Rachel. Each scenario was tested: an officer pulling a child through the window, another lifting and carrying her out, and others attempting to exit through the front door.

The grim choreography of these re-enactments led Woite to a chilling conclusion. The abductor likely possessed considerable physical strength, standing at least five feet nine inches tall, necessary to navigate the window's high ledge and manoeuvre a struggling child. The most plausible method, disturbingly, involved reaching in through the window and pulling Louise out directly—an act that would require considerable strength and startling audacity.

Yet, this theory raised more questions than it answered. How had no one heard a sound? Rachel had been only an arm's length away, her small form undisturbed. Colin and Dianne's bedroom was mere metres down the hall, doors ajar. The house, quiet enough to hear a child's sigh in sleep, had betrayed no sound of struggle, no muffled cries piercing the night.

This silence haunted Woite. It led to unsettling possibilities. Had Louise been drugged, rendered helpless before her abduction? Or, in a scenario that seemed to defy belief but could not be dismissed, had she left willingly? As the investigation pressed on, the questions hung in the air, heavy and unanswered.

**South Australia in Flames**

**February 16, 1983** — The investigation into the disappearance of Louise came to an abrupt halt as the state was devastated by catastrophic bushfires, later known as Ash Wednesday. The first of the fires was only 20 kilometres south of Hackham West at McLaren Flat. Fires broke out across regions, including the Adelaide Hills, Eyre Peninsula, South East, and the Mid-North, burning over 200,000 hectares, destroying 383 homes, and claiming 28 lives—17 of them volunteer firefighters. With temperatures soaring to 43°C, low humidity, and strong winds, the fires spread rapidly, catching many off guard.

Poor communication and a lack of modern technology worsened the chaos. A State of Emergency was declared for the first time in South Australia's history. Though the fires were contained mainly by the next morning, thanks to cooler weather and light rain, flare-ups continued for weeks, and damages totalled an estimated $204 million.

**The Pyjama Top**

**February 28, 1983.** Four weeks after the chilling telephone call from the abductor, Ms S noticed something peculiar on her front lawn. At first glance, it appeared to be nothing more than a discarded piece of rubbish, an oddity she dismissed as she walked her son to school. But upon her return, the item remained exactly where she had seen it—undisturbed, conspicuously neat against the uneven grass. Curiosity piqued; she picked it up.

It was a child's pyjama top, neatly folded both lengthways and crossways, as if someone had deliberately placed it there with care. Seeing it gave her pause, but she was unsure of its significance. She carried it to the back of her house, placing it in an empty pot plant container near the rubbish bin, intending to forget about it.

However, as Ms S went about her morning chores, an unsettling thought crept into her mind. She recalled a newspaper article mentioning that Louise Bell had been wearing a summer-weight pyjama top when she disappeared. Could this be connected?

Unable to shake the feeling, she retrieved the top from the pot, inspected it more closely, and then, driven by a gnawing sense of dread, placed it on her kitchen bench atop a shopping bag to avoid further contamination. With trembling fingers, she dialled the police.

"You wouldn't believe what I just found on my front lawn," she told the detective who answered.

"What?" came the quick, sharp response.

She described the garment: "kid's size 10," "orangey floral."

The detectives recognised it instantly.

"Stay where you are. We are on our way."

The abductor was playing a cruel, psychological game, taunting both the grieving parents and the desperate police.

Within minutes, Detective Lyn Strange arrived at Ms S's residence. He carefully examined the bright orange piece of clothing, lifting it gently towards his face.

"The smell was fishy, marshy," he later described—a damp, decaying odour that clung to the fabric.

Detective Strange placed the pyjama top into an evidence bag and drove straight to the Bell home. Colin Bell's hands shook as he examined the torn, dirty garment. His eyes locked onto a familiar detail: a small, crudely cut-down red label near the neck.

With a voice barely above a whisper, Colin said, "I cut it off because Louise complained that it irritated her. It's Louise's top."

Tears welled in his eyes, blurring his vision.

Detective Strange placed a comforting hand on Colin's shoulder. No words were exchanged—none were needed. In that devastating silence, the grim reality settled over them: Louise was likely no longer alive.

South Australia's Chief Forensic Scientist, Walter Roemer, meticulously examined the pyjama top. He tape-lifted materials from the surface using adhesive tape, pressing the tape gently against the fabric and transferring them to glass slides. Five tapes per section covered the front, internal front, back, and internal back.

The analysis yielded a crucial clue: algae and soil particles embedded in the fibres. The forensic report was precise—the samples were consistent with those found in a river estuary. The Onkaparinga River became the new focal point, a mere few minutes' drive from the Bells' home.

Police wasted no time. They established a search headquarters in a derelict farmhouse near the riverbank. STAR Force officers, alongside local volunteers, combed the area with painstaking detail. Clad in waders, twenty officers trudged through the muddy banks, their eyes scanning for any trace of Louise.

Divers plunged into the murky, shallow waters, battling thick, black mud that sucked at their movements and obscured visibility. The river gave up none of its secrets easily.

After a week of exhaustive searching, hope waned. Nothing was found. The river remained silent, its dark waters refusing to reveal Louise Bell's fate.

**Cat and Mouse**

The brazen act of phoning a neighbour of the Bells and then planting evidence for the police to find is significant in interpreting the motivation driving this criminal. It was as if he believed he had an intellect far superior to the police detectives and that he could never be outsmarted. It was as if this cruel abductor was playing a cat-and-mouse game with authorities, secure in the knowledge that he would always stay one step ahead of them.

When the abductor phoned Ms S, he described the police as 'stupid' in not noticing things, which was a clear indication that his ego was out of control and extremely dangerous. Not only had he found satisfaction with the abduction, but he was now enjoying the challenge of the chase.

His behaviour screamed 'Psychopath'. He fitted the tag perfectly. Psychopaths tend to have a grandiose sense of self, are pathological liars with skill in manipulative behaviours, lack remorse, lack empathy, and fail to accept responsibility while believing social regulations do not apply to them.

Was he really interested in Louise's welfare, or was he only interested in getting pleasure out of more publicity for his ghastly crime? In giving Ms S the phone numbers of media outlets, he was clearly a self-absorbed monster. The way he described in detail Louise's injuries to Ms S had overtones of someone enjoying himself ... a sadist.

The painful reality was that Louise was not suffering from an ailment... but was deceased at the hands of this evil, murderous man.

## A letter of pain

During February, the Bell family had wanted Louise's birthday to be kept secret. However, they decided to speak to the media to obtain publicity and increase awareness. Colin Bell held a birthday card in his hand as he talked about the trauma the family had endured. Fighting back tears, he said softly, "Tomorrow is Louise's birthday, and she will be 11 years old. We have not heard anything from her since she went missing. We have had no positive sign whether she is alive or dead.

"The pyjama top, the earrings, and the telephone call have been no real indication to us of her welfare.

"We ask that the person or persons responsible make contact. It does not have to be to us or the authorities.

"This person must have a brother, a sister, a mother, or a friend ... someone who knows but has not come forward."

Colin Bell had recently attempted to return to his employment, but it didn't last; he decided to remain at home on leave to assist the police investigation and to support his wife and younger child, Rachel.

"I just want her to come home so we can be a family again."

Colin Bell penned a public plea to the abductor that was published in the two major newspapers in South Australia:

## Part One  Chapter 4  February 6, 1983

"To the person who has taken our daughter, Louise, it is very difficult to put into words the nightmare that is happening to us since Louise has been gone.

We feel at times that this is not really happening, but that feeling doesn't last long, and reality soon returns. It is a physically sick feeling as well as mental torture, a nightmare that will not end.

She has never hurt anybody; we just want Louise, so we can be a whole family again.

Rachel misses her sister and her friend very much. She is lost without her. Please bring her back and stop this torture.

Why don't you phone us and tell us where we can find her? She means so much to us. Just let someone know where they can find Louise. We miss her so much.

We do not have a lot, but what we do have is love for our girls, Louise and Rachel.

If you can help us, ring Father Aitken 51 2551

I also feel for you.

If you have children of your own, you would understand what we are going through.

If you don't have any children, I can't describe to you the anguish we are feeling.

If you have lost someone dear to your heart, and you may have taken our Louise to help replace your loss, believe me, it will not bring your loss back.

I will ask you to look at Louise and think, could you possibly hurt this little girl anymore, by keeping her from us, any longer?

You know Louise can be a loving child; you must have found that she is everything we say.

Please, if not for anything else, let her get medical attention and let her go so she can bring happiness back to us and many others who know and love her.

PS Please tell her we love her always.

## Chapter 5

# Vital Clue

March 9, 1983—Detective Supt Edwards, in charge of the Major Crime Squad, released a statement to the media in which he announced that a new lead had the "potential to be the most promising information in the case to date." He said the police had intensified their investigations over the past week due to fresh information from a member of the public.

"Police artists are preparing a composite photograph of a man who may be able to help our inquiries.

"I do not wish to elaborate further because it could prejudice our inquiries."

A day later, the police released a photo of the suspect's identity.

A witness described the man police were seeking in connection with the abduction of Louise Bell as about 183 cm (6ft), with blond collar-length hair, clean-shaven, of athletic build, and between 20 and 30. He was wearing a light-coloured shirt, blue jeans, and brown boots.

**Wiggly Ears**

One of Australia's most outstanding investigative journalists, Dick Wordley, wrote a powerful piece in The Bulletin that captured how far South Australian Police were willing to go in their search for Louise Bell.

Among the dedicated officers was Dennis Isaacs, a policeman known for a simple, endearing trick—he could wiggle his ears. It was a small gesture that managed to bring a flicker of joy to children in a time of deep fear. Eight-year-old Rachel Bell, Louise's younger sister, remembered him not just as a policeman, but as "the nice man who wiggles his ears," someone who made her smile despite the shadows hanging over her family.

But Isaacs wasn't there to entertain. There was nothing light-hearted about his visits. Though some children had started playing again in the small park and on the quiet sidewalks of Hackham West, no one played alone anymore. Parents were cautious. Bedroom windows stayed shut, and doors remained locked even through the suffocating summer heat. The sense of safety had vanished, especially in the Bell household.

Rachel, usually shy and now visibly anxious, had spent hours with Senior Sergeant Isaacs at the nearby Christies Beach station. She responded to his gentle manner, especially the ear-wiggling, and felt safe to talk. She told him everything she could remember. But that wasn't much.

She recalled going to sleep beside Louise in their shared bedroom and waking up alone. Her sister was gone—just gone.

## "Kinksville"

The tragedy of the missing Hackham West girl had once again highlighted Adelaide's reputation for bizarre crimes. Adelaide finally started to question itself.

The provocative wordsmith, Max Harris of the Sunday Mail, wrote an article titled "Use your eyes to save our city." He asked his readers, 'Is Adelaide, Kink City, Australia?'

Harris outlined the terrible murders and disappearances that had plagued the 'City of Churches'. Adelaide was only just getting over the horrible crime of the Truro murders, where five young women were abducted from the city streets and then murdered. Adelaide was then stunned by the macabre murders of five young men, which became known as The Family murders.

"It all adds up over the years to give South Australia a national reputation as a place where numerous homicidal kinks and psychotics proliferate beneath the middle-class respectability of the place. It's time we all started asking some pertinent questions. Firstly, is the 'Kinksville' generalisation true, or is it merely that bizarre crimes cause more public agitation in a community as small as ours?"

Harris asked his readers to be aware of their surroundings. "If you see something, ACT!"

**"We've Got Him"**

In the quiet of their home, the Bell family was once again shaken by the weight of the investigation. Throughout those harrowing months, Major Crime detectives maintained a steady presence, keeping the family informed, their voices a constant source of reassurance. But on a hot November day in 1983, it was clear something had shifted. Several task force members arrived at Dianne and Colin's house with urgent news. Colin looked through the lounge room curtains as the detective approached the front door.

The air was thick with anticipation as a senior detective, his voice low but steady, finally broke the silence. "We've got him." The words hung in the room like a heavy fog. The parents of Louise, already worn from months of grief, collapsed into each other's arms, the tears they had long kept at bay finally pouring out.

No stranger to the painful weight of such news, the detective explained that an arrest was imminent. They had someone in their sights, and the end was finally within reach.

For Colin Bell, the news sparked an eruption of emotions. A man who had always kept his anger in check now could not contain his boiling rage. His calm but strained voice would later be heard on television as he spoke of his feelings. "I'm like Mt St Helens," he said, "smouldering and ready to explode. There are times when the poison of hate comes out, and other times you must suppress it."

His grief was compounded by the memory of his father, who had passed away only weeks earlier. In a moment of raw honesty, Colin revealed that he had confessed something haunting in his father's final days. "He told me how he cheated death in the South Pacific during the war and asked me why it couldn't have been him instead of Louise."

Then, on November 28, 1983, the day finally came. The man they had been hunting appeared in a special court hearing, charged with the abduction and murder of Louise Bell. A suppression order was in place, meaning his name was not immediately revealed to the public. But police were confident. Forensic evidence was on their side, and everything pointed towards one man: Raymond John Geesing.

Geesing—a tall figure with brown, wavy hair and a neatly trimmed beard—stood in the courtroom, his face a mask of silence. The police presented evidence they believed firmly linked him to the crime. A pair of sneakers, found in his car, matched fibres taken from Louise's pyjama top. And there was more. Geesing had lived in the Hackham West area at the time of the abduction, a stone's throw away from Ms S, a woman who had received a call from the abductor. To her horror, Louise's pyjama top had been found on her front lawn.

As the detectives' details painted a chilling portrait of the man before them, it was clear: the investigation was not over, but this was the beginning of a new chapter. In this chapter, justice for Louise Bell might finally take shape.

**Savagely Beaten**

A week after the initial court hearing, the case against Raymond John Geesing was once again set to unfold. But this time, the atmosphere in the courtroom was different. The accused child murderer was not present. His absence was explained by his lawyer, who solemnly informed the court that Geesing had suffered severe head injuries. He was, the lawyer stated, still recovering from a brutal beating that had occurred at the Adelaide Gaol—a beating so savage, it would reverberate throughout the case.

According to reports, up to seven inmates had viciously attacked Geesing during a meal break at the prison. Geesing was found unconscious on his bunk—his body battered; his head covered in blood. Officers had rushed to his upstairs cell after hearing the sounds of a violent struggle, but by the time they arrived, the damage had already been done. Geesing lay gravely injured, barely clinging to life.

The details of the assault were chilling. Geesing had been beaten with a steel bar from a weightlifting set, a wooden stool and makeshift weapons that caused massive trauma. His lawyer described the attack as "draconian," a word that barely captured the brutality of what had transpired. Prison officials had launched an investigation, questioning the other inmates about the attack, but the truth seemed elusive, buried under layers of silence.

The injuries Geesing sustained were catastrophic. His head was fractured in multiple places, and emergency craniofacial surgery was required to try to save him.

But despite the violence he had endured, Geesing was not forgotten. On December 12, he was brought back to court—his appearance had altered so significantly that it was as though he were a different man altogether. The front half of his scalp had been shaved to reveal a 15-centimetre-long scar running from the front of his left ear. His left eye was swollen and nearly shut, his nose was bent, and his face was a patchwork of fading bruises. His shoulders slumped forward as if the weight of his crimes—and now his injuries—had broken him. His gaze was fixed on the courtroom floor, as though he could not bear to meet the eyes of anyone who might look upon him.

He no longer resembled the man who had once entered the courtroom with a look of defiance. Now, he appeared as a beaten, broken figure—both inside and out. The judge, noting his condition, remanded him in custody until March 5, 1984. Geesing would face the consequences of his actions, whether in court or in the harsh reality of prison life.

## Hidden in plain sight

Raymond Geesing's name had surfaced early in the investigation. A detective from Christies Beach Police Station had reached out to the team working on Louise Bell's disappearance with a disturbing tip: years earlier, Geesing had been charged with an offence against a child. He walked free—not because he was found to be innocent, but because of a legal technicality.

That was enough to put him squarely on the detectives' radar. They began tracing his movements, zeroing in on where he'd been the night Louise vanished. Every detail, every gap in his story, was scrutinised.

When it came time to search his home, Detective Madden turned his attention to Geesing's vehicle—a Ford station wagon. As fate would have it, Madden owned the very same model. He knew its quirks intimately, including one most people wouldn't notice: when the back seats were folded flat, a carpeted flap could be lifted, revealing a hidden compartment.

As Madden reached in his fingers brushed against something soft. He pulled out a pair of old, dusty sneakers—tucked away, as if deliberately hidden. Geesing had no explanation for why his shoes were hidden. He proclaimed his innocence and believed his ex-wife was setting him up.

To Madden, it wasn't just a pair of shoes. It was another whisper from the shadows, another clue that Geesing had more to hide than anyone yet knew.

Scientific analysis of the debris on the soles of the shoes matched the debris from Louise's pyjama top.

## The Truth

Detective Madden hadn't expected much when he followed up on a message from Raymond Geesing's ex-wife. It was a routine lead—just another loose end in a case with far too many. She had mentioned, almost in passing, that when Geesing was thrown out of the house, his belongings were given away. Among them was an old, unremarkable wardrobe.

Madden tracked it down. A man on the outskirts of town had taken it off her hands and shoved it in his back shed, forgotten and gathering dust. It was the kind of task that could easily be dismissed as a waste of time, but in the investigation into the disappearance of Louise Bell, there was no room for assumptions.

Inside the wardrobe, Madden sifted through the debris of a former life—dog-eared books, mould-speckled magazines, yellowed papers. Then something caught his eye: a folded piece of newsprint wedged tight behind a warped panel. Carefully, he prised it loose.

It was a double-page spread from *The Truth* newspaper. His breath caught as he scanned the bold headline. It was a detailed account of the abduction of Eloise Worledge, the little girl snatched from her bedroom in Beaumaris, Melbourne, back in 1976. The circumstances—so eerily similar to Louise Bell's—sent a chill crawling up Madden's spine.

Coincidence? Maybe. But to Madden, it felt like something darker. A hidden obsession. A sinister breadcrumb in a trail of guilt that seemed to lead, more and more, back to Raymond Geesing.

The noose around Geesing was tightening. One by one, the pieces were falling into place—damning evidence piling up like a landslide he couldn't outrun. Then came the call that sent a chill through the investigation room: several inmates at Adelaide Gaol had come forward. They wanted to talk. And they wanted to talk about Geesing's involvement with Louise.

## Chapter 6

# The Geesing Trial

On November 9, 1984, the trial of Raymond Geesing for the abduction and murder of Louise Bell began in the South Australian Supreme Court, known as the Sir Samuel Way Building, formerly 'Moores', a magnificent old department store.

At 37, Geesing stood accused of committing one of the most heinous acts imaginable, and the courtroom was filled with anticipation as the Crown laid out its case.

Prosecutor Apps began by detailing Geesing's life in the months leading up to the tragic event. Between June 1979 and November 1982, Geesing had lived with his wife and stepchildren on Hagen Crescent, Hackham West—only a stone's throw from the Bell family's home. For three years, his life had intersected with that of Louise and her family, though it would only be after he moved away, two months before the abduction, that his connection to the Bell family would come to light.

The prosecution's case was primarily circumstantial, relying heavily on testimony from inmates who had shared time with Geesing while he awaited trial. As Apps opened the proceedings, he recounted a conversation that took place within the grim walls of Adelaide Gaol in April 1983. One inmate, it seemed, had confronted Geesing.

"You knocked that little kid, didn't you?" the man had asked.

To the horror of those within earshot, Geesing allegedly replied with a simple "Yes."

Moments later, the prisoner turned on him, and the inmate viciously beat Geesing.

But the chilling revelations didn't stop there. According to Apps, Geesing later confided in a prison officer, claiming that he had been set up for Louise's murder by his wife and her lover. And in yet another twist, there were whispers of an alleged alibi being arranged by another prisoner. However, perhaps the most disturbing detail was Geesing's admission to another inmate. Geesing reportedly said he was "a bit frightened" about the woman who saw him take the child.

Being an alleged child killer made life in prison hell for Geesing. He was constantly harassed and threatened. There is an unwritten creed among inmates of prisons worldwide: paedophiles/child killers are not to be tolerated; they are looked upon as the lowest of the low. In recent years, there have been measures taken to protect these criminals, but in the early 1980s, child molesters had to take their chances among the general prison population. It didn't take long for Geesing to find enemies.

The prosecution's case continued to build with the testimony of the first of 80 witnesses—Louise's parents, Colin and Dianne Bell. Dianne, visibly shaken, took the stand and relived the heart-wrenching morning of January 5, 1983. Her voice trembled as she described how she had woken to find her daughter's bed empty. The night before, Louise and her sister, Rachel, showered and went to bed around 8:30 pm. Dianne and Colin had settled in to watch television, and by 10 pm., they were preparing for bed. Dianne had checked on the girls; Rachel was asleep, but Louise was still awake. She had asked Louise to shut the curtains before returning to her room.

The doors to the girls' room and the hallway were open, as always. But when Dianne awoke at around 6 am, the world as she knew it shattered. Louise was missing. Dianne noticed the damage to the wire screen on the window. The curtains were parted, and the window was wide open. Her heart pounded as she called out for Colin. Together, they searched the house, but Louise was not there. It wasn't long before the police were called.

As Dianne wiped away her tears on the stand, the magnitude of what had been lost was clear. Their daughter was gone, and they were determined to find the man who had taken her.

Colin Bell's voice cracked with emotion as he was asked to identify his daughter from the last known photograph of the missing schoolgirl. The photograph, taken with a camera Louise had received for Christmas, had been impounded by police so the film could be processed. As the picture was handed to the jury, Colin described his daughter as shy, quiet, and close to her family.

"She was a very shy girl in the presence of people who were strangers," he said. "School formed a very important part of her life. She was happy; she enjoyed school."

He spoke fondly of their time together as a family over the holidays. Christmas had been a joyful occasion, and they had taken several trips, even planning to see the film E.T.

Louise had been especially excited about it after seeing a trailer at the Colonnades shopping centre.

The day before her disappearance, Colin explained, they had spent time at Noarlunga Shopping Centre, returning home for lunch before heading back out later that afternoon. They had their evening meal, watched television, and then Colin left the house briefly to check on a property he was looking after. It was a routine and typical day, until it wasn't. And now, his world would never be the same.

## "You knocked that kid, didn't you?"

Possibly the most damaging evidence against Raymond Geesing came from a fellow inmate named Browne, who had been in close quarters with Geesing at Adelaide Gaol. In April 1983, while both men worked together in the prison kitchen, tensions were already high following a visit from detectives investigating the disappearance of Louise Bell. As Browne and other prisoners Flynn, Marshall, and McGinnes stood together discussing Geesing and the case, Geesing was only a few metres away, seemingly oblivious to the conversation unfolding around him.

But Browne's voice cut through the air, loud and deliberate. "Geesing, you're a kid fucker, and the jacks have got you for Louise Bell," he yelled.

Geesing, though he glanced towards the group, said nothing.

Browne, undeterred, repeated the taunt: "Geesing, come over here."

When Geesing did not move, Browne took matters into his own hands, walking towards him, pointing a finger directly in front of Geesing's face. "You knocked that little kid, didn't you?" he demanded.

There was a heavy and suffocating silence for a moment before Geesing's head lowered, his voice barely audible as he responded, "Yes."

The words were spoken with such quiet resignation that Browne's punch was no surprise. The blow landed squarely on Geesing's cheek, sending him crashing to the ground. Prison guards rushed in to restore order, but the damage had been done. Browne's words and Geesing's admission would echo in the minds of those who heard them for months to come.

As chilling as that moment was, it was not the only incriminating conversation from Geesing's time behind bars. Another former inmate, Morris Thomas Phipps, testified about his conversations with Geesing regarding the disappearance of Louise Bell. Phipps recalled asking Geesing if he had an alibi for the night of Louise's abduction.

Geesing, perhaps too comfortable with the inquiry, responded that he had been at a woman's house that night, minding her property. He claimed a church member had called him, providing the excuse that seemed almost too rehearsed. But Phipps wasn't buying it and offered to sell Geesing an alibi.

"How much would it cost?" Geesing asked, his curiosity piqued. Sensing an opportunity, Phipps replied that the price would be $500. According to Phipps, Geesing appeared to give the offer a great deal of thought, as though the idea of covering up his tracks was not foreign to him.

The conversations between the two men didn't end there. On another occasion, Phipps claimed that Geesing had asked about the possibility of obtaining protection while in prison and what kind of sentence he might face if he were to clear up the matter.

Phipps bluntly responded, "You'll get life," and suggested that the parole period would likely be something in the ballpark of twelve years.

During another conversation, Phipps made a shocking claim. He said that Geesing, aware of his chemistry background from working at Uniroyal Tyres, had once asked him whether it was possible to create a chemical solution that could dissolve a human body. According to Phipps, Geesing replied that it was possible—but added that human hair was the most difficult part to eliminate.

As the trial progressed, Phipps revealed yet another disturbing conversation: he had urged Geesing to clear up the matter for the sake of Louise Bell's parents. "For their sake, clear it up," he said.

Geesing, after a moment's pause, had responded with chilling indifference. "The only thing I can't do," he told Phipps, "Is take them to the body."

These supposed conversations, full of strange confessions and careful denials, made Raymond Geesing look guilty. Of course, most of this was based on what the other inmates claimed happened.

## "I have the police beaten on this one."

Another prison witness, McConnell, said he overheard Geesing conversing with another prisoner, Craig. He claimed Geesing boasted, "I have the police beaten on this one." McConnell added that Geesing indicated he was a bit frightened about some woman who had seen him "take the kid". Geesing then asked Craig "How do you think I'll go?" Craig replied, "I don't know, but if I were you, I would keep your fucking mouth shut." According to McConnell, Geesing "appeared to go a bit white and then blushed".

The witnesses against Geesing were piling up, but did they have credibility? History has shown that inmates have often used their hearsay evidence to gain freedom from prison or a reduction in an upcoming trial. The use of prison inmates as witnesses in such a serious charge was fraught with danger, but Major Crime detectives believed their stories. They were adamant that Geesing was the killer, even though they had virtually no direct evidence.

## "You wouldn't be as good as Louise."

Another strange twist in the trial came from Ms G, a former female Army reservist. She told the court she had attended an Army Reserve course at Hampstead Barracks for two weeks, which began on January 15, 1983. During the second week of the camp, she and three other female recruits were having a conversation about sex in the mess hall. She said Geesing had joined the conversation for about half an hour. Ms G said they had all been joking and another reservist, Ms T, had "said a few things to Private Geesing". "As we were leaving, Geesing turned around and said, 'You wouldn't be as good as Louise'". She also said Geesing had mentioned another name but had not heard it. After his alleged comment, she said she had turned around, and Geesing seemed "a bit frustrated."

Under cross-examination, Ms G revealed that she had received medical treatment at the camp earlier that day. She had been given a tablet for stomach cramps, but after taking it, she had felt depressed and acted stupidly. She returned to the regimental aid post, where someone had told her she had been given the wrong tablet. Ms G also admitted she might have had a drink containing rum that evening in the mess.

## Pyjama Top

Witness Ms S was called to give vital evidence about Louise's pyjama top, left on the front lawn of her Hackham West home. She told the court that on February 28, 1983, she had collected her milk and paper at about 6.45 am from the front porch of her house and had seen something towards the footpath edge of the lawn. At about 8.45 am, she had walked her son to school and noticed the item in the same position on the lawn. It was still there when she returned, so she picked it up and eventually took the child's pyjama top inside.

Detective Lynton Strange told the court that when he saw the pyjama top on a table in Ms S's home, it was dirty and ripped, and the lace had been unstitched in a specific area. Strange said the garment had a "Fishy, marsh-like" odour.

Prosecutor Apps explained that forensic scientists had examined Louise's pyjama top, and that foreign material, including green algae, shell, and some silt, had been found. Scientists who gave evidence asserted that such material would have come from an estuarine environment. Such an environment was found where the Onkaparinga River met the sea – an area not far from the Bell home. It was also an area that Geesing frequented, his favourite fishing spot.

When police examined a pair of Geesing's sneakers found hidden in his car, a similar type of estuarine silt was found on the soles. A detective told the court, "There was nothing to say the silt had come from the Onkaparinga, but it could not be excluded."

Hardly a smoking gun, but why were Geesing's shoes hidden in his car?

## Geesing's Alibi

Geesing first came to the attention of the police during the early stages of the investigation. Detective Anderson of Christies Beach CIB told the court that on Sunday, January 9, 1983, he spoke to Geesing at a house in Mitchell Park. He told Geesing he was inquiring about Louise Bell's disappearance and that they would like to search the house. After Geesing said, "All right," they searched the entire property but found nothing relevant. Geesing, who cooperated with the search, told Anderson that on January 4, he was at a friend's home in Edwardstown and returned home about 5 pm, where he had tea.

Geesing said, "I went next door with a bottle of wine, which I shared with a neighbour. I left there about 10 pm, came home and went to bed."

Geesing's behaviour towards detectives during questioning was, at best, unconvincing. Detective Strange said that during a short conversation with Geesing at Adelaide Gaol, Geesing had been "very nervous" and had taken deep breaths several times and "licked his lips as if his lips were dry." A short time later, Geesing had agreed to have a tape-recorded interview with him. During that interview, Geesing retracted his previous statement. Geesing said he had thought about that statement and remembered that the drink with the neighbour had been on the following night. He said that the night Louise disappeared, he had stayed home and watched TV alone.

## Geesing takes the stand

When Raymond John Geesing took the stand to be questioned under oath, he understandably looked tense. He repeatedly wiped his brow as beads of perspiration formed on his forehead. When grilled by Prosecutor Apps, Geesing was forthright in denying all the allegations made by the prison witnesses.

Apps: The prisoner never said, 'Geesing you knocked that little kid didn't you'.

Geesing: No

Geesing again denied having been told by a prisoner, "The jacks have got you for Louise Bell." When asked if a former inmate had hit him on any occasion in the gaol, Geesing replied "No."

"Did anything like that happen?"

"No."

Raymond Geesing's testimony before the jury was a tense and calculated affair. When questioned about his frequent visits to the Onkaparinga River, Geesing casually admitted to fishing there "quite a few times." Still, his answers were far less convincing when it came to the discovery of his sneakers hidden in a void in his car. Geesing claimed to have no idea how the shoes ended up in that particular spot, a statement that seemed less than truthful under the scrutiny of the courtroom. He explained that the sneakers, which had been worn for fishing, crabbing, and basketball, were simply left behind when he moved out of his matrimonial home in November 1982. He claimed they had been relegated to a shed because of their poor condition. So, how did they end up hidden in his vehicle?

His explanation only raised more questions. When asked about the shoes' strange hiding place, he struggled to provide an answer that matched the facts, and the jury was left to wonder: Were these just old, worn shoes, or was something darker at play?

Geesing's testimony grew even more strained when the topic turned to his knowledge of chemicals. Asked about his former work with dangerous substances, he admitted that some of the chemicals he handled "may have been corrosive." But when pressed further about a conversation with an inmate regarding the ability to dissolve a body with a chemical mixture, Geesing vehemently denied it. He claimed he didn't know enough about chemicals to comment on whether any could be used to render a body unrecognisable. However, he acknowledged that certain chemicals he worked with "gave off toxic odours" and could be harmful if inhaled over time. But when asked about chloroform or other chemicals that could render someone unconscious, Geesing remained adamant that he had never had access to such substances.

But it wasn't only his knowledge of chemicals that would come under scrutiny. The prosecution, aware of Geesing's background, began to zero in on his Army Reserve training, particularly his understanding of "voice frequencies" and "voice tones". These concepts had been discussed about radio transmissions, and the prosecution saw a connection between Geesing's knowledge of these technical details and the chilling phone call made to Ms S on January 17, 1983, by the man who had abducted Louise. The caller had warned Ms S that he would not speak to authorities or the press because his voice could be traced using technology. He even mentioned "voice tones" and "voice frequencies"—details that would interest someone familiar with radio transmissions.

Geesing denied discussing such matters with anyone, claiming he had only attended lectures about voice frequencies during his Army

Reserve training. Still, the jury could not ignore the eerie parallel between the caller's words and Geesing's military background.

Then Geesing dropped a bombshell that strengthened the prosecution's case. He claimed he had received a brief phone call from Louise's father, Colin Bell, sometime in September 1982. The call, he said, lasted no more than three minutes—but that short conversation would later cast a long shadow, raising troubling questions about Geesing's ties to the Bell family and his role in the mystery of Louise's disappearance. At the time, Geesing was Chairman of the Hackham West Community Association and had previously visited the Bell home to recruit Colin into the group.

Finally, Prosecutor Apps cornered Geesing with a blunt question: Had he called Ms S on January 17, 1983?

"No, definitely not," Geesing replied, but his vehement denial only heightened the suspicion hanging over him. Each word he spoke seemed to tie him further to the darkness surrounding Louise Bell's tragic fate, and the jury would have to decide whether those denials were merely the words of a desperate man—or the truth.

## "Worthless piece of evidence"

The evidence against Raymond Geesing was mounting, even though much of it was circumstantial. It painted a picture that, while not entirely conclusive, was starting to take shape—one that cast a shadow over the father of four. Still, his defence lawyer, Mr Duggan QC, refused to let the case against his client stand unchallenged. In a blistering attack on the prosecution's case, Duggan accused the Crown of weaving a "sinister scenario on a foundation of nothing."

He described the case as "worthless," its evidence "thin," and many of the witnesses as "absolutely hopeless."

Duggan's rhetoric grew more pointed as he targeted the statements of prison inmates—testimonies crucial to the prosecution's argument. To Duggan, these claims were nothing but "inconclusive," "absolute drivel," and "wild speculation". He went as far as to suggest that some of the evidence might have been "tampered with" or even fabricated entirely. The former prisoners, Duggan argued, had been trying to trick Geesing into admitting his guilt. Their hostility towards him was palpable, and Duggan warned the jury that relying on such evidence was "dangerous". He urged them to consider the inconsistencies between witnesses, implying that this was not simply a matter of unreliable memories but of deliberate manipulation.

But the Crown, led by Prosecutor Mr Apps, wasn't ready to back down. In his closing remarks, Apps implored the jury to consider the circumstantial evidence as a whole, rather than as isolated fragments. "There comes a time," Apps said, "when common sense and understanding revolt and reject mere coincidence. There comes a time when you say, 'come on – enough is enough.'" He pressed the jury to remember that Geesing had the opportunity to commit the crime. He could have easily left the woman's house that night, travelled to Hackham West, and abducted Louise Bell.

The prosecutor also called attention to a phone call received by Ms S on January 17, 1983. The caller had claimed the call was random, but Apps countered that it was more likely the caller had chosen to reach out to Ms S because he knew his voice would be unrecognisable, while Colin Bell would have easily identified him. According to Apps, this proved that the call was not a mere crank call. The jury was urged to consider the caller's awareness of voice tones and how this might link back to Geesing's military training, particularly his knowledge of radio transmission and voice frequencies.

As the trial wound down, one of the more bizarre twists came when Ms S revealed that she had undergone hypnosis to recall the details of the man she had seen watching her shortly after the abduction.

Justice Cox cast doubt on the accuracy of the testimony, stating that her description did not seem to match Geesing. Moreover, the court was unsure if the description even referred to the time she had found Louise's pyjama top. The jury was left to ponder whether the hypnosis had truly uncovered anything valuable or had merely muddied the waters further.

After six gruelling weeks, the jury deliberated for over 24 hours before returning with their verdict: Guilty of murder and Guilty of abduction. The courtroom fell into a tense silence as the foreman announced the decision. Three women jurors were visibly distressed, with one breaking into sobs.

Geesing, standing in the dock, flinched at the verdict and closed his eyes as the weight of the decision settled in. He was led away to the cells; his future was now bleak. He was terrified of the inmates awaiting him back at the Adelaide Gaol.

Geesing's mother, devastated by the news, broke down in tears. In stark contrast, Colin and Dianne Bell were surrounded by their friends, finally receiving the long-awaited confirmation that the man responsible for their daughter's disappearance had been held accountable. Yet, there was no sense of relief for the Bells—not until they could find Louise.

Colin Bell spoke of the battle that was far from over. "We are still going to have to live with it," he said. "But now that the blame has been squarely laid at his feet, perhaps we can find where Louise is."

Despite the verdict, Geesing's solicitor vowed that the fight wasn't over. He promised a relentless appeal, one that would test the legal system in ways that South Australia had never seen before. However, as the dust settled on the courtroom battle, a darker revelation emerged: Geesing had been convicted only a month after Louise's abduction of six counts of unlawful sexual intercourse with a 14-year-old girl and one count of indecent assault.

For the police and the public, the conviction of Raymond Geesing was a hard-won victory, a long-awaited solution to a case that had haunted the state for months. But the lingering question remained: Had they truly got the right man? The cases of other missing children—Jane, Arnna, and Grant Beaumont, Joanne Ratcliffe, and Kirsty Gordon—still hung in the air like unfinished business. For the public, the truth was clear enough: Raymond Geesing had been found guilty, but the war to find justice for every missing child was far from over.

**The Aftermath**

After the verdict, detectives who worked on the Bell case started tying up the final threads of the Geesing trial. There was a collective sense of relief among the team—relief that their relentless efforts had finally brought some measure of justice for the Bell family. There were times they worked throughout the night to arrest the killer of Louise.

But that calm was suddenly interrupted when a phone call came through to Detective Paul Madden.

## Part One  Chapter 6  The Geesing Trial

On the line was Michael McConnell—the former inmate who had first come forward with damning information about Geesing. His voice was strained, urgent. He wanted to meet, but not at police headquarters. Instead, he insisted on the Central Market—neutral ground.

Detective Paul Madden wasn't your typical cop, not by the standards of the era. He was tough, when necessary, but there was something else—an openness, a quiet empathy—that allowed people from all walks of life, even those with criminal backgrounds, to talk to him openly. Maybe it was his honesty. Perhaps it was that he didn't judge.

Madden had joined the force as a teenager and completed the police academy with solid marks. However, not everyone believed he was suited for frontline work. One senior officer had once told him bluntly, "Paul, you'll do fine in most areas of policing—but I'm not sure how you'll handle an arrest."

The reason? Madden was rail-thin—almost fragile in appearance. According to the academy sergeant, he lacked the physical presence for the rough-and-tumble side of the job. But what Madden lacked in size, he made up for in something far more valuable—instinct, intelligence, and an ability to earn trust from people others couldn't reach.

His compassion for Adelaide's inner-city downtrodden wasn't just part of the job—it was a calling. At one point, due to the quirks of police shift work, he found himself living a double life: by day, volunteering at a homeless shelter; by night, working as a detective. It was a demanding balance, but one he embraced wholeheartedly. For Madden, justice didn't stop at arrests—it extended to understanding, dignity, and giving people a second chance.

As Detective Paul Madden made his way through the noise and

chaos of Adelaide's Central Market, unease settled over him. He couldn't shake the question: why had McConnell insisted on meeting here, in public, away from the safety of the station? At first, Madden assumed it was another tip-off. But the moment he caught sight of McConnell's face—pale, tight with anxiety—he knew this wasn't routine. This was serious. Possibly catastrophic.

They shook hands. Madden ordered two coffees, then sat down, bracing himself. McConnell didn't waste time.

"I lied," he said. "Everything I told the court about Geesing—it was all made up."

The words hit Madden like a punch to the temple. He was stunned. His mouth went dry. For a moment, he just stared at McConnell, unable to speak.

The walk back to police headquarters felt like a marathon. When Madden stepped into his sergeant's office, the look on his face said it all. Moments later, he was on his way to the Director of Public Prosecutions.

## Chapter 7

# The Geesing Appeal

April 1985 — The courtroom was steeped in anticipation as the Geesing appeal commenced, the air thick with tension. It wasn't just another day in court; it was the day when prisoner-turned-witness Michael McConnell unravelled a narrative that had once fortified the prosecution's case against Geesing. Now, he stood ready to dismantle it.

The courtroom buzzed with the kind of sensational revelation that feeds headlines and haunts the public conscience: McConnell wanted to retract his damning testimony against Geesing. McConnell spoke with a voice that sometimes quivered, not from fear of the courtroom's authority, but perhaps from the weight of his conscience. He claimed that ever since the trial, a relentless, gnawing guilt had shadowed him, compelling him to tell the truth.

McConnell took the stand with solemnity, his oath echoing in the hushed courtroom. He swore that the pivotal incriminating conversation he had allegedly overheard between Geesing and another prisoner, Craig, had never happened. The foundation of his original testimony began to crumble under the scrutiny of cross-examination.

McConnell recounted how, shortly after the trial, he had contacted Geesing's senior counsel and solicitor, driven by a need to confess his deceit. He had then approached Detective Sergeant Madden, admitting that his earlier testimony had been fabricated. According to McConnell, the lies were not born from personal vendetta but rather from manipulation—he claimed prisoner Browne had coerced him into weaving this false narrative. However, McConnell's clarity wavered under the intense glare of courtroom interrogation. His story shifted subtly, and he began to backpedal, suggesting that Browne had not explicitly instructed him to lie.

The courtroom watched, rapt, as McConnell described his relationship with Browne. "When I arrived in prison," he stated, "Browne told me that Geesing was a 'dog.'" In the bleak lexicon of prison life, a 'dog' is a betrayer, a snitch—an identity that could mark a man for life, or worse. Browne had convinced McConnell that Geesing was not only a so-called dog but also guilty of the unthinkable: the abduction of Louise Bell. The two men had shared an eighteen-year history of friendship and alcohol-fuelled camaraderie, a bond that made McConnell susceptible to Browne's fervent conviction and shared disdain for "kid fuckers", as they crudely termed them.

Significantly, McConnell had first implicated Geesing only days after his release from prison in November 1983. Intoxicated, he had stumbled into a police station and claimed that Geesing feared "a woman had seen him take the kid." He later provided two official statements: the first conspicuously devoid of this claim, and the second, crafted with the damning detail included.

Now, in the appeal, McConnell recanted two critical elements of his testimony: (1) Geesing's alleged confession, "I'm a bit frightened that some woman saw me take the kid," and (2) the assertion that Geesing had visibly blushed and turned pale when McConnell supposedly overheard him discussing his legal prospects with another inmate.

The Crown was unambiguous about the stakes. Without McConnell and Browne's testimonies, their case against Geesing would wither, and it would be insufficient to convince either the original jury or any future panel in a retrial.

In a signed affidavit provided to Geesing's solicitor, McConnell wrote, "The lies I have mentioned were things I was told to say. I was asked to tell these lies by Trevor John Browne... I was first asked by Browne to tell these lies about a week after I went to the Adelaide Gaol in September 1983."

Yet, on the stand, McConnell seemed almost desperate to dilute Browne's influence. He insisted that Browne had not explicitly ordered or directed him to fabricate the story. At one point, he even suggested that Browne might not have asked him at all. Still, he conceded that Browne had concocted the tale, and he had perpetuated it, driven by a twisted mix of loyalty, contempt for Geesing, and his moral decay.

The cross-examination was relentless:

Q: You now say you made that up?
A: Yes. I heard something about a woman. That was Browne that told me that.
Q: Browne told you that?
A: Some woman had seen him take the kid or something like that.
Q: But you say you did not hear it yourself?
A: Not from Geesing.
Q: Browne told you that Geesing had said that?
A: Yes.

Browne's eyes followed McConnell's every word, his posture rigid with indignation. The courtroom's tension spiked when Browne took the stand in rebuttal. He vehemently denied fabricating the story or instructing McConnell to present it as truth. Outside the courtroom, the two men engaged in clandestine conversations and even shared drinks, a bizarre camaraderie that muddied the waters of credibility.

Following the original trial, McConnell's conscience had seemingly betrayed him to others as well. He began receiving anonymous threats: menacing phone calls, chilling notes urging him to "keep his mouth shut." The threats escalated to violence—a rifle shot fired in the direction of McConnell and his de facto wife served as a grim warning to stay silent about the Louise Bell case.

Through the tangled web of deceit and retraction, one unsettling truth emerged: prisoners had actively baited Geesing, dangling the prospect of alibis, coaxing him into incriminating conversations—a calculated entrapment strategy.

Yet, despite the risks and the threats, McConnell recanted. He stood before the court, risking perjury charges, driven by a fractured conscience and the fragile hope of redemption. Though riddled with contradictions and evasions, his testimony carved deep holes in the case against Geesing, leaving the courtroom to grapple with the elusive nature of truth itself.

On 12 April 1985, the South Australian Court of Criminal Appeal unanimously upheld an appeal by Geesing. Chief Justice, Mr Len King, ruled that Geesing's 1983 trial had been a miscarriage of justice, and its guilty verdict against Geesing for the murder and abduction of Louise Bell must be set aside.

Justice King said that the prisoner informants were unreliable and untrustworthy witnesses. The Court of Criminal Appeal ordered no retrial, and Geesing walked to freedom after serving seventeen months in prison. During this time in prison, he suffered facial scars after several vicious attacks on him by inmates. He later received a compensation payment for his injuries.

When the decision was handed down at 9.55 am, Geesing left the dock and sat in the body of the court, with his head bowed, shedding tears. He was a free man. Later outside the court, Geesing told awaiting reporters, "Justice has been done ... I have the Lord on my side."

Geesing celebrated his release from custody by lunching with his solicitor and a private detective. His mother, Mrs Gladys Geesing, said, "He is on top of the world. I don't believe he should ever have been put in gaol. I knew he never did it." Mrs Geesing wept joyfully at her modest Torrensville home after his release. She said his second marriage had ended while he was in gaol. She and three of his four children from a previous marriage had continued to visit him during the 17 months he was in prison. "They told the youngest girl that her dad had gone. The eldest child had to change schools and change her name because of teasing from other children over her father's imprisonment. Today, Ray is on top of the world."

Neighbours shielded a distraught Dianne and Colin Bell after learning of the decision and didn't comment to the media.

The police were publicly silent on the court's decision, but privately, the detectives who had worked on the case were seething with disappointment. The investigation into the Louise Bell abduction was back to square one. The only suspect they knew of was found to be innocent in the eyes of the law.

A terrible mistake had been made, although Geesing was back in prison 25 years later after being found guilty of unrelated child sex charges.

Police and the South Australian community were asking the same question. 'If Geesing didn't do it, then who the hell did it?'

The Bell family was devastated at the realisation that their little girl's killer was still at large. The detectives who worked on the case got a frosty welcome when they knocked on the door of the Bell home and revealed the news of Geesing's successful appeal. The torment of the abduction, followed by the failed prosecution, was too much to bear for Louise's parents. What seemed like a closure to their nightmare turned out to be another distressing ongoing ordeal.

The Major Crime Squad had put all their efforts into prosecuting an 'innocent' man; they had no other suspect, nor a plan B. The killer of Louise Bell was enjoying the fruits of freedom... for now.

## Chapter 8

# "I am worried about Eloise..."

When the mystery caller (Louise's abductor) rang the Hackham West resident, Ms S, regarding the welfare of Louise Bell, he let slip a vital piece of information that contributed to an extraordinary puzzle. The caller referred to Louise as 'Eloise'.

"I am worried about Eloise... I mean Louise."

The slip was subtle, but unmistakable. Did the caller—Louise Bell's abductor—reveal something critical, or was it an intentional red herring? South Australian detectives assigned to the Bell case suspected the latter, a calculated attempt to divert their attention across the border into Victoria. There, in 1976, another little girl had vanished under chillingly similar circumstances.

Eloise Worledge had been eight years old when she disappeared from her home on Scott Street, Beaumaris, a bayside suburb 20 kilometres south-east of Melbourne's CBD, a mere 500 metres from the beach. It had been the night of January 12, during the school holidays, and her abduction had left investigators baffled. The case had gone cold, leaving a gaping wound in her family's life and an enduring mystery in Australian crime history.

At first glance, the Worledge home had appeared stable, but

cracks had long been forming beneath the surface. Eloise's parents, Patricia—known as Patsy—and Lindsay Worledge had been married for nearly a decade, but by 1976, their relationship was irreparably fractured. They remained under the same roof for the sake of their three children, yet they lived largely separate lives. Lindsay, a New Zealander and respected lecturer at Caulfield Institute of Technology, was deeply immersed in his Master's studies at Monash University. He was methodical, serious, and a man devoted to academia. Conversely, Patsy was the opposite—vivacious, social, an artistic free spirit who had once taught art but now focused on raising their children. The Worledge couple were looked upon as "chalk and cheese".

Eloise, the eldest, was a shy but bright girl, intensely creative like her mother. Though reserved and prone to asthma, she had recently begun to emerge from her shell through Brownies and an art club called the Hubble Bubble Club. She was set to start grade four at Beaumaris Primary School after the summer holidays. Her younger siblings, Anna (6) and Blake (4), adored her, and the family moved through their daily routines like any other—until that terrible night.

If the mystery caller had truly mistaken Louise for Eloise, the implications were staggering. What if it hadn't been a simple slip of the tongue? What if the cases were not only similar but connected? What if the man who took Louise Bell had also stolen Eloise Worledge seven years earlier?

The possibility was as haunting as it was terrifying.

This was either a slip of the tongue or an attempt to create a smokescreen by the abductor.

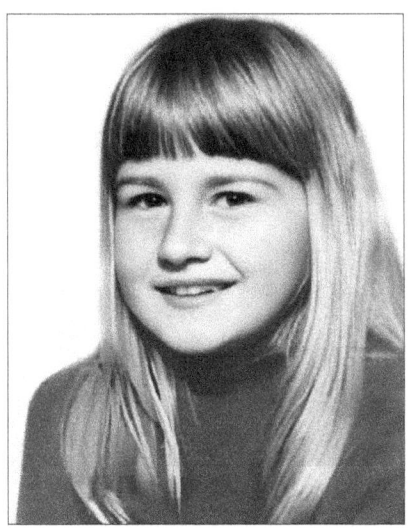

*Eloise Worledge*

But what if it wasn't a deliberate smokescreen by the abductor? What if Louise's abductor had also snatched Eloise?

**"Eloise's Room"**

January 10, 1976, was supposed to be a night of celebration for Patricia "Patsy" Worledge, who was marking her 33rd birthday. A party was being held across the street at a neighbour's house, but Lindsay Worledge didn't expect an invitation. He had been distanced from the crowd for a while, but the deliberate exclusion still stung. Humiliated and furious, Lindsay spent the night pacing up and down Scott Street, seething as he checked the registration of every car parked at the house.

When Patsy finally came home at 2 am, her husband was waiting. He was drunk and emotional, unable to hide his hurt. The arguments that followed were explosive. Their screaming filled the night air for two long hours, echoing in the quiet suburban neighbourhood. But by morning, the rage had been replaced by regret. The couple, weary and ashamed, began speaking civilly, as if the violent outburst had never happened. They both knew their behaviour had gone too far. The cracks in their marriage were too deep to ignore, and Lindsay agreed it was time to start looking for a place to live on his own.

Lindsay took the children to the beach for a swim and ice cream the following day, trying to make up for his behaviour. They needed something to break the tension—something to remind them of the good in their family. But the air was thick with unspoken truths. The marriage was hanging by a thread.

By Monday, Lindsay had put on his professional face. He was a guest speaker at Honeywell Securities. After a lunch with an executive, he returned to the institute around 2:15 pm, where the quiet of the summer break made for a relaxed afternoon. Lindsay joined a few colleagues at a nearby hotel for drinks, and by the time he returned home around 5 pm, the house felt peaceful. Dinner was served, and they ate as a family, talking and laughing through the meal. Afterwards, Lindsay played board games with his children while Patsy, content in her own world, busied herself with her crafts.

It was around 8:15 pm when Patsy dressed for her jazz ballet class. She kissed the children goodnight, and Lindsay ensured they were all safely tucked into bed by 8:45 pm. But as the house settled into silence, Eloise, their eldest, couldn't sleep. At 9:15 pm, she quietly slipped out of bed, went to the kitchen for a glass of milk, and joined her father in the lounge. The two sat together, quietly talking. Perhaps in a moment of vulnerability, Lindsay decided it was time to explain the state of their marriage to Eloise. He wanted her to understand that the split was for the best. Sensing the gravity of the conversation, Eloise snuggled close to her father as he spoke.

At 10 pm, Lindsay told his daughter it was time for bed. He kissed her on the forehead, and Eloise returned to her room.

When Patsy arrived home shortly after, she was in and out, collecting a dress she was working on to show a neighbour. She returned home again at 10:30 pm, but later told police that she had forgotten to lock the front door. The outside porch light was off, and the front flywire door was closed but not secure. Still carrying the weight of the evening, Patsy thought about locking the door but let the thought slip away. At 11 pm, she took some ironed clothes and placed them in Anna and Blake's rooms before entering Eloise's room. She straightened the covers on her daughter's bed, kissed her, and went to bed herself.

Lindsay, still watching TV, turned off the television around 11:40 pm and headed to bed. He told police he checked on the children before settling in. But Patsy, in her statement, said this was unusual. It was a nightly ritual for one of the parents to turn off the hallway light for the children before they went to bed. But that night, the light remained on. It was the first crack in the familiar routine—a subtle but telling shift.

At 4:45 am, Patsy woke to use the toilet. The house was quiet, but she noticed something unsettling—the passage light was now off. The thought barely crossed her mind as she went back to bed.

The following morning, Lindsay rose around 6:30 am. As he walked to the kitchen for a drink of water, he noticed that Eloise's door was shut. He didn't think much of it, assuming she was still asleep. He went outside briefly to retrieve the milk and newspaper, returning to the living room to read. It wasn't until Anna and Blake came into the room that he heard the unsettling words from his four-year-old son: "Eloise is not in her room."

Lindsay didn't take the comment seriously. But the unease lingered.

At 7:30 am, Patsy went into Eloise's room. Lindsay would later describe hearing his wife's voice shriek in horror: "Eloise!" Rushing to her side, Lindsay saw his wife trembling, staring into the empty room. They both turned to the window. The curtain had been pulled aside, and the flywire screen was cut. The window was wide open.

Panic set in. Lindsay immediately contacted the police, his voice eerily calm as he reported the break-in. But as he explained, the only thing missing was his eight-year-old daughter. The terror of those moments—when reality slipped into something far darker—would haunt Lindsay for the rest of his life.

Within minutes of Lindsay's frantic phone call, the Beaumaris police were on the scene. Sergeant Davies, an officer with decades of experience, arrived quickly, taking in the sight of the cut flywire screen. His instincts, honed over years of responding to frantic calls from distressed parents, told him this was different. He'd seen many cases where children had wandered off, only to be found unharmed within hours. But this time, something felt wrong. The scene was too calculated, too unsettling. This was not a simple case of a child running away.

The window in Eloise's room had been forced open to a gap of only 38 centimetres—barely wide enough for a child to squeeze through, let alone an adult. But it wasn't the open window that unsettled investigators the most. The torn flyscreen told a more disturbing story. It had been sliced and rolled up from the inside, an anomaly that sent a chill through the detectives. At a height of 195 centimetres, it was nearly impossible for someone, especially a child, to manipulate it without a ladder.

Yet what lay beneath the window sent an even darker message. The ground was covered in seemingly harmless bark chips until officers noticed those same bark chips scattered inside Eloise's room. It felt too deliberate, too staged. The so-called break-in could have been nothing more than a red herring, meant to throw investigators off track.

Detectives shifted their focus. What if the abductor had entered through the unlocked front door? The scene bore the markings of careful orchestration. It was not a frenzied snatch-and-grab, but a chillingly precise abduction.

In the hours that followed, the Worledge family was questioned. But it was Blake, Eloise's four-year-old brother, who provided a clue that would haunt the detectives for years. He whispered in a small, solemn

voice, "I heard a crackling noise." He had been too frightened to look, but the implication was clear—someone had moved through the room, their footsteps crunching on the sea-grass flooring—someone who didn't belong there.

A task force of 15 detectives was immediately assembled, led by Detective Superintendent Fred Warnock. A father of five, Warnock projected steady confidence despite the weight of the case bearing down on him. Facing the media, he assured the public that Eloise would be found. But behind the scenes, investigators knew they were in a race against time.

The search that followed was one of the largest in Melbourne's history. Up to 250 police officers searched Beaumaris and the surrounding areas. They knocked on doors, questioned neighbours, and followed every potential lead. But as the days bled into weeks, hope began to dim. No trace of Eloise surfaced.

One particularly unsettling lead involved a young door-to-door

*Lindsay and Patsy Worledge*

salesman who had been seen lurking around the neighbourhood before Eloise vanished. Witnesses recalled him as "cocky," too persistent. One neighbour, only two blocks from the Worledge home, described how the man had asked unsettling questions about school children. "He was hiding behind walls and that sort of thing," the neighbour remembered uneasily. For a moment, detectives thought they had their man. But after thorough background checks, the salesman was ruled out—another dead end.

With every passing day, the case slipped further from their grasp. Theories swirled, suspicions mounted, but concrete evidence remained frustratingly out of reach. The abduction of Eloise Worledge was unlike anything Victorian Police had ever encountered. And despite their best efforts, they were no closer to knowing the truth.

Four days after his daughter vanished, Lindsay Worledge was called in for questioning by Melbourne detectives. The experience, he would later describe, as nothing short of terrifying. As the hours wore on, he maintained his innocence, even offering to take a lie-detector test to prove his sincerity. But he was not the only one under suspicion. His wife, Patsy, and several neighbours and family members were all looked upon with suspicion. The tense and bitter marriage between Lindsay and Patsy had become fodder for the rumour mill. The whispers of a family in turmoil had fuelled the investigation, with police wondering if the answer to Eloise's disappearance might lie closer to home than they wanted to admit.

As Melbourne buzzed with rumours and innuendo, one thing became clear: this was no ordinary case. And the truth—whatever it might be, remained frustratingly out of reach.

In the wake of Eloise's disappearance, Lindsay and Patsy sought solace and answers from unlikely sources. Desperate, they turned to clairvoyants, hoping for a glimpse into the truth. They also underwent lengthy hypnotherapy sessions in an attempt to unlock any buried memories that might shed light on what had happened to their daughter. But still, there was no breakthrough; no revelation.

Months passed, and the weight of uncertainty only grew heavier. Detective Superintendent Warnock, who had overseen the initial investigation, publicly came to Lindsay's defence. In an attempt to quell the whispers and suspicions swirling around the Worledge family, Warnock addressed the media. "A lot of people think he has acted callously," he said. "He's not the sort of person who wears his heart on his sleeve. Deep down, he cares about his children." But no matter how much the detective reassured the public, the haunting absence of answers left lingering doubts in the minds of those who had been watching closely.

As police investigators sifted through hundreds of leads, new and troubling details began to surface. The night Eloise disappeared, the quiet neighbourhood of Beaumaris had been anything but peaceful. At 10:00 pm on January 12, a neighbour of the Worledges heard what he thought was a prowler outside his home. The following morning, he discovered that his tool shed had been ransacked, with items strewn haphazardly around the yard.

Other neighbours reported seeing a green Holden station wagon creeping through the streets with its lights turned off, adding to the growing sense of unease. But it wasn't until midnight that a witness saw something that made the hair on the back of her neck stand up.

A young man ran across the street, darting in front of her car before disappearing onto the Worledge property. It was a chilling sight, but what followed would prove even more unsettling.

Around 2:00 am, another neighbour heard the unmistakable sound of a child crying at night. The cry was followed by the sharp, unmistakable sound of a car door slamming shut. It was a detail that would stay with her, etched in her memory.

Despite the growing collection of evidence, the case remained open. As with all unsolved crimes, the police kept it in the back of their minds, always waiting for that crucial piece of information that might bring the truth to light. In cases involving child abductions, police take a proactive approach, continuously revisiting the investigation, especially when new information arises.

**Cruel Hoax**

In 1995, nineteen years after Eloise was taken, the past collided with the present in a sterile courtroom in Melbourne. Kenneth Benfield, now 36, from Mildura in north-west Victoria, stood accused—not of abducting Eloise, but of something almost as cruel: sending an obscene ransom note to her grieving family in the weeks following her disappearance. The note, crude and vile, had demanded $10,000 from Patsy Worledge, Eloise's mother. Signed simply "Fred," its language hinted at horrors no parent should have to imagine.

The courtroom air felt heavy as the yellowed, aged ransom note was tendered into evidence. It was a relic from a time when hope had still flickered, however faintly. But the actual shock came not from the words on the page, but from the fingerprint it carried—a match, police said, to Kenneth Benfield.

Sergeant Terry Claven, a fingerprint expert, took the stand with the quiet authority of someone who has spent years tracing the faintest ridges and patterns that human skin leaves behind. He explained that it was during a routine review of cold cases in July of the previous year that Benfield's fingerprint surfaced. It was, he testified, "beyond reasonable doubt" that the print belonged to Benfield. And yet, that print had gone unnoticed for nearly two decades, despite previous attempts to find a match.

"I can't explain why it wasn't identified earlier," Sergeant Claven admitted under cross-examination. "It's one of those things we will never know."

Technology had changed, of course. A fingerprint-matching computer system, introduced in 1987, had eventually caught what human eyes had missed. Benfield's fingerprints had been in the database since then, quietly waiting for the day when past and present would collide.

But here was the cruel twist: police did not believe Benfield had anything to do with Eloise's abduction. His crime, it seemed, was of a different kind—an opportunist exploiting a family's unimaginable pain, adding another layer of torment to an already unbearable tragedy.

In a statement read aloud, Patsy Worledge recalled the flood of letters that had poured in after Eloise disappeared—some offering sympathy, others riddled with malice. This note had been one of the worst, not only for its vile content but for the false hope it dangled, however grotesquely.

Magistrate Jelena Popovic listened, her expression unreadable, before ordering Benfield to stand trial in the County Court.

**Coroner's Inquest**

In 2004, the Melbourne Coroner's Court held an inquest into the death of Eloise. At the inquest, Detective Nazaretian revealed that despite Eloise's father, Lindsay, being the prime suspect at the time of her disappearance, a 2001 investigation found no evidence to implicate either of Eloise's parents as the culprit.

Nazaretian said evidence suggested someone had staged the scene to make it appear as if the flywire screen had been cut from the inside, thereby averting suspicion from people connected to the Worledges.

He believed, "The motivation to cut the screen from the inside by an intruder with no connection to the household seemed inconceivable." Nazaretian was adamant that "Entry, exit or both was most probably made through the front door, which Ms Worledge said she had left wide open."

The inquest took a sideways tack when personal details were aired that revealed Lindsay and Patsy Worledge were both having extramarital affairs at the time. It was claimed that Mr Worledge was "To move out of the house the day Eloise went missing." Senior Constable Nazaretian described this circumstance as "striking in its timing".

Nazaretian read from his notes regarding a 2002 interview with Ms Worledge. Patsy Worledge told the police officer that her husband at the time "Was involved in the disappearance as a means of prolonging the inevitable and as a way of spiting her".

Police left no stone unturned in their search for the abductor/

killer. Bizarrely, at one point in time, two of Patsy Worledge's female friends and even her sister were under the spotlight. Still, these investigations ended without any evidence whatsoever being produced against the women.

The Coroner, Mr Hender, was adamant that Eloise would not have left home voluntarily. He believed the information gathered by police, such as a neighbour's account of hearing a child cry out and a car door slam at 2 am on the night of the disappearance, was significant in his findings.

"It is not possible on the evidence to find who the person or persons responsible or when and how Eloise met her demise, but her disappearance and presumed death remain suspicious."

## February, 2024

Nearly five decades after Eloise's disappearance, the school she had attended in 1976 again made headlines.

Beaumaris Primary School, once a picture of suburban tranquillity, found itself at the centre of a harrowing investigation when the Victorian Government launched an inquiry into the sexual abuse of children by teachers. The following revelations would shake the foundation of the state's education system.

ABC reporter Russell Jackson investigated this morbid story. One survivor told him, "It was mind-boggling." Another said it was "beyond belief."

A lawyer representing the victims didn't mince words. "It was calculated. It was covered up—just like in the Catholic Church."

For decades, allegations had swirled, but after six months of exhaustive inquiry, a formal investigation delivered its findings to the Victorian governor. What emerged was a pattern of shocking abuse—and an institutional effort to protect perpetrators rather than children.

The inquiry exposed a damning truth: the Victorian Education Department had knowingly shuffled known paedophile teachers from school to school, putting countless children in harm's way. However, the investigation's scope was narrowly defined, focusing on a cluster of offenders at Beaumaris Primary, located in Melbourne's idyllic bayside south-east.

Beaumaris Primary was chosen as the inquiry's focus due to the sheer volume of abuse that took place there in the '60s and '70s. Four prolific offenders overlapped at the school during the early '70s. Yet they weren't only confined to Beaumaris. Throughout their careers, they were quietly transferred between 24 Victorian government schools, spanning four decades.

Among them was Grahame Steele, an imposing former football star who allegedly preyed on children for decades, both on school grounds and at a secluded holiday home in Inverloch. Survivors fought for years to have Steele charged, while he remained employed in the education system from 1952 to 1990. He died in 2013, never facing justice. Evidence presented at the inquiry suggested Steele continued to offend even after being reported to police.

Then there was Darrell Ray—the most infamous of the Beaumaris predators. As the school's librarian and sports coach, Ray wielded unchecked power. In the '60s and '70s, he systematically abused boys at four state schools and within the St Kilda Football Club's Little

League, where he coached for over a decade. His crimes finally caught up to him in 1979 and again in 2001, when he was convicted of 33 offences against 21 boys. But the damage had long been done.

Ray's brother-in-law, Gary Mitchell, was another name survivors would never forget. For his entire 31-year teaching career, Mitchell assaulted boys under his charge, despite credible complaints from students and parents as early as the 1970s. Gaoled multiple times since 1996, Mitchell was also named as an abuser of young footballers in the St Kilda Little League. Like Ray, he left a trail of victims at Beaumaris Primary.

However, the story of David MacGregor truly laid bare the extent of the Education Department's complicity. MacGregor's crimes spanned three decades before he finally faced charges in 1985. Even then, the department shielded him. He remained employed, was granted new teaching positions, and was only removed from the classroom in 1992, thanks to the intervention of headmasters and the teachers' union, rather than the authorities.

During the Beaumaris inquiry, Victorian Education Department deputy secretary David Howes admitted it was "distressing to read" how MacGregor's case had been handled. But his words revealed an even darker truth. "The department's attention seems to have been primarily about where MacGregor wanted to go," Dr Howes stated. "It was only a question of where to move him—nothing about how to protect the students at that school immediately."

The nightmare at Beaumaris Primary was not an isolated tragedy. It was a symptom of a much larger, insidious epidemic that had infiltrated

Victoria's government schools. And as the inquiry concluded, it was painfully clear: the system had protected the predators, not the children.

* * *

The disappearances of Louise Bell in 1983 and Eloise Worledge in 1976 remained among Australia's most haunting and baffling child abduction cases. Although separated by seven years and occurring in different states, the similarities between these two cases are too striking to be ignored.

Both abductions took place during the long, hot Australian summer school holidays—January, a time when routines were disrupted, families took vacations, and neighbourhoods grew quieter. Both girls vanished in the dead of night, seemingly plucked from the safety of their bedrooms without a sound. There were no cries for help, no evidence of a struggle, no shattered glass or overturned furniture. In the morning, their families awoke to an unfathomable horror—an empty bed, a missing child, and no clear answers.

Perhaps most chillingly, both abductions bore the hallmarks of a calculated, precise operation. The perpetrator had to be familiar with the house and understand its vulnerabilities. There were signs of tampering with the bedroom window screens in both cases—a careful, silent intrusion rather than a chaotic break-in. Both homes were located close to the children's schools, suggesting a predator who stalked his victims beforehand, learning their habits, their movements, and the rhythm of their lives.

These eerie parallels did not go unnoticed by law enforcement.

In 1983, after Louise Bell's disappearance, South Australian police contacted their counterparts in Victoria, requesting the case files on Eloise Worledge. The similarities were impossible to dismiss, and investigators considered the possibility that the same perpetrator could be responsible for both crimes.

But could there be another explanation? One dark possibility is that Louise's abduction was a copycat crime. Eloise's disappearance had received widespread media attention across Australia, and the terrifying notion of a child being taken from her bed had lodged itself into the nation's collective consciousness. Did Louise's abductor draw inspiration from Eloise's case? If so, what does that say about the nature of this offender—someone who not only preyed on innocent children but also sought to replicate an already unsolved and notorious crime?

Then, there is the broader question of whether these cases form part of an even larger pattern. The 1973 abduction of Joanne Ratcliffe and Kirste Gordon from the Adelaide Oval—two little girls who vanished without a trace—has often been theorised to have connections to the infamous Beaumont children's disappearance in 1966. Could the same predator, or a network of like-minded offenders, have been at work across Australia for decades?

It is, of course, speculation. There is no hard evidence linking these cases together beyond their disturbing similarities. And yet, when a predator successfully takes a child without being caught, it emboldens them. They refine their methods. They become ghosts in the night, their presence known only by the gaping absence they leave behind.

So, the question lingers: Was the monster who took Eloise the same one who took Louise? If not, was one inspired by the other? Until we have definitive answers, we are left with a trail of eerie coincidences, unanswered questions, and the lingering, haunting possibility that a single predator may have stolen not just one, but multiple children, leaving behind grieving families and a nation desperate for justice.

# PART TWO
# Michael Black

*Michael Black*

## Chapter 1

# 18 January 1989

Michael Black was an adventurous 10-year-old. He could sometimes be a little cheeky, but he was always respectful to others, especially adults. He wore a brilliant, toothy smile and had a warm, sunny disposition. His mother lovingly described him as a ragamuffin.

Living in the country town of Murray Bridge (75km SE of Adelaide) was ideal for such an outdoor-loving boy. Apart from the River Murray, which ran alongside the township's centre, there was also abundant open space for bush walking and discovery.

After having lunch at his father's home (his parents had separated), Michael gathered his fishing gear as he was going to cycle down to the banks of the River Murray, a ten-minute ride. The trip was a special milestone for Michael, as it was the first time he had been permitted to venture to his favourite fishing area without his father's company. David Black sat Michael down at the kitchen table and gave him strict instructions on where he could and could not go that afternoon. Their relationship was strong. He gently touched his son's shoulder and specifically told Michael not to cross the bridge. "It's too dangerous with the traffic, just enjoy yourself along the Sturt Reserve area."

David knew Sturt Reserve was always well populated in summer with fishermen and campers—plenty of locals to keep an eye on his boy.

David Black smiled proudly as he watched his son pack his fishing gear onto his BMX bike. The sun was shining, and the air smelled fresh as Michael balanced his fishing rod with a bag of tackle slung over his shoulder. His loyal companion, Bessie—a seven-year-old red retriever—was by his side, eager for their afternoon adventure.

"Here," David said, handing Michael some twine. "If the dog-catcher comes along, tie Bessie up with this." He then slipped $2.50 in coins into Michael's pocket. "Here's some change for a drink and chips."

David added with a loving pat on the head, "I'll pick you up after work if you're not home by then."

Michael nodded; his face flushed with excitement. After that, he rode off down West Terrace, his fishing rod and bag carefully balanced. The river was only a kilometre away.

"Call me if you need anything!" David shouted, though the distance swallowed his words as Michael's bike wheels clicked down the road. Michael waved but didn't turn back.

Sturt Reserve was a popular spot for locals and visitors alike. The lush, green grass and towering river gum trees provided plenty of shade for anyone wanting to spend a few quiet hours fishing or having a picnic. For the children, there was the famous Bunyip, a mechanical monster that roared to life when activated by a coin, drawing a delighted laugh from every child who saw it.

For David and Michael, the reserve was their sanctuary, a place where they could bond and reconnect with each other. They would often fish together at twilight, preparing their catch over a simple barbecue as they shared the quiet joy of the moment. A successful accountant, David spent his weekdays buried in spreadsheets, but the weekends were his time to escape. The outdoors had always been his passion, one that was passed down to him by his father, a well-known bushman. David's love for nature ran deep, and it was a bond he shared with Michael, a boy who revelled in the quiet beauty of the world around him. A bit of a loner, Michael preferred his own company, finding peace in fishing, exploring, and bird watching, always with Bessie by his side.

By the time David closed his office door at 4:00 pm, an unsettling feeling had begun to take root. Michael was never late—dinner was a routine, a given. But as the clock crept past 5:00 pm, unease tightened its grip. Something wasn't right.

Turning to his daughter, Alley, he said, "Let's check the river." It seemed like a minor worry at first—maybe Michael had lost track of time, caught up in the quiet thrill of fishing.

But as they reached Sturt Reserve, dread overcame David Black. The area was eerily still, nearly deserted. There was no sign of Michael. No bike. No fishing rod. No dog.

David's voice took on an edge of urgency as he stopped strangers, his words tumbling out faster each time: "My son—dark brown hair, about this tall—had a dog with him. Have you seen him?"

Each shake of the head, each blank stare, sent a chill through him. Michael was nowhere. And suddenly, David knew—this wasn't just a boy losing track of time. Something was dreadfully wrong.

Panic began to claw at David's chest. He told Alley to stay in the car, and he jogged down the riverbank's edge, eyes scanning the area desperately.

"Michael, where are you?"

His thoughts raced, but the knot in his stomach tightened with each passing minute.

David drove to Michael's grandmother's house, scanning the front yard for any sign of him. Nothing. Not a glimpse of the boy. The seconds felt heavier now, each one swallowed by a growing unease.

At first, there had been irritation—Michael was late, and that was unlike him. But the feeling shifted quickly, replaced by a cold edge

## Part Two  Chapter 1  18 January 1989

of worry that sharpened with every passing minute. Soon it was something darker: alarm.

He drove slowly through the neighbourhood, each turn of the wheel deliberate, his eyes sweeping the footpaths, the parks, the verges. Street after street passed without a trace of Michael. Every so often, he looped back home, his gaze flicking instantly to the spot by the back shed where the boy's bike should have been. It was always there—until tonight.

David's chest was tight, his pulse quickening, but he forced his voice and his hands to remain steady. His young daughter sat beside him, watching, trusting. He couldn't let her see the fear that was building inside him, couldn't let it spill over and feed her own. So, he swallowed the panic, fixed his eyes on the road ahead, and kept driving.

By 6:45 p.m., David's restraint had crumbled. He returned to his home and called the police, his words clipped and tight. "This isn't like Michael," he told the officer. "He's never this late." The truth hung between them, heavy and unspoken: something was seriously wrong.

He then rang the local hospital, his heart pounding as the receptionist checked the admissions list. But no child had been brought in that afternoon. The line went dead, leaving only the hum of the receiver—and the creeping certainty that this was no ordinary delay.

Overcome with fear, David couldn't sit still. Panic then set in. He bolted to the nearby police station, his heart pounding with every stride. He burst through the doors and rushed to the front desk.

"Please," he begged the officer, his voice shaking. "My son is missing— something's terribly wrong. You have to help me. Please, send someone right away."

His thoughts spiralled into terrifying possibilities — what if his son was hurt? Lost? Trapped somewhere and unable to call for help? The not knowing was unbearable, and the silence only deepened his dread.

Within minutes, officers were dispatched to the area around Sturt Reserve. David was instructed to return home and wait by the phone.

An hour passed. Then came the call. It was the police. David gripped the phone, his knuckles white, as the officer spoke. "We've found Michael's bike and fishing gear at Thiele's Reserve," the voice said.

David froze. His stomach dropped. Thiele's Reserve? That was four kilometres away — on the other side of the river. His mind reeled. "No… no way would he have gone there," he stammered, his voice cracking. "That's not where he was supposed to be."

Then came the detail that made David's blood run cold. The officer said Michael's belongings were found neatly arranged, as if someone had carefully placed them there.

A deep chill swept through David. His heart pounded with a father's worst fear — that something wasn't just wrong… it was deliberate.

"Michael is notoriously untidy," David told the officer. "He never would've left his stuff like that."

Tears filled David's eyes as the crushing truth began to sink in. Michael hadn't just wandered off. This wasn't a simple mistake or a moment of distraction. A cold dread gripped his chest, and deep within his soul, he knew his son was in grave danger. He didn't just think it. He felt it, raw and urgent, in every fibre of his being.

The late afternoon sun cast long, golden shadows across the riverbank as police officers moved with grim efficiency, their footsteps muffled by the soft earth beneath them. Michael Black's bike was the first item they found, its small frame leaning neatly against a wooden railing near the water's edge. Next to it, as if carefully arranged, lay his fishing rod and haversack. His rubber thongs were placed side by side, and his shorts folded neatly, as if their owner had every intention of returning shortly. However, Michael was nowhere to be found, although his best friend, Bessie, was there.

When officers reached for Michael's belongings, the dog's reaction was instant—hackles up, teeth bared, a low, guttural growl that stopped them cold. Then, without warning, she bolted, loping along the riverbank, nose to the ground, following a scent only she could sense. Minutes later, she reappeared, circling back as if drawn by an invisible tether. She lowered herself beside Michael's abandoned thongs, let out a deep, shuddering sigh, and rested her head on them, guarding them like a final vigil. In the end, a police officer managed to coax her into a vehicle, taking her to Michael's mother's home.

A chill crept over the officers as they took in the scene. There was an unsettling sense of order to it all.

Michael's shirt was discovered beside the public toilet, only metres from the water, snagged high in the branches of a gnarled willow tree along the upstream boundary of the reserve. A tragic drowning seemed the most immediate and logical conclusion. An urgent call was placed to the police aqualung squad.

Back at his home, David Black sat in his dimly lit living room, his gaze constantly focused on the silent phone on the side table. His heart lodged somewhere between hope and an unspeakable fear. The sharp crunch of tyres on gravel outside snapped him to attention. He rushed to the window, his pulse quickening. A car had pulled into his driveway. His estranged wife, Margaret, stepped out, her face etched with worry. The blur of red fur caught David's eye—Bessie, Michael's faithful dog, leapt from the car and bounded towards him.

David met Margaret halfway, and the two embraced with the desperation of parents grappling with a nightmare they couldn't wake from. Margaret had been scheduled to take the children that day, but work obligations had forced her to ask David for one more day—a simple request, one that now echoed with cruel significance.

That morning, David had slipped back into work mode after three precious weeks with his children. His day was crowded with meetings and client calls.

Bessie pressed against David's legs, whining softly. David knelt to inspect Bessie. Physically, she was unharmed, but her demeanour was off. The usually calm and gentle dog was restless and agitated, her nose to the ground and tail down, emitting low, anxious whines.

"She was fired up," David later recalled. "Sniffing everywhere, pacing. She never acted like that, especially not at night."

Then David noticed the frayed twine still attached to Bessie's metal choker collar. It was the same twine he had handed Michael earlier that afternoon, meant to secure Bessie if needed. David measured the length, noting how it aligned with Bessie's back teeth. She had chewed through it to escape. Later that evening, police discovered a matching piece of twine tied to a tree stump not far from where Michael's shirt had been found.

By 8.30 pm, darkness had swallowed the landscape. The river's gentle current whispered under the cold beam of flashlights. SES

## Part Two  Chapter 1  18 January 1989

volunteers fanned out along both banks, their torches slicing through the oppressive gloom. Two police dog handlers moved methodically through the underbrush, searching for any clue, any sign. Portable floodlights bathed the area in an unnatural glow, transforming the tranquil reserve into a chaotic hive of activity. The close-knit community had mobilised swiftly, dozens of volunteers converging with a singular purpose: to find Michael.

Michael's mother arrived at the river with her brother, her face pale, eyes wide and unseeing. She was overwhelmed by the sheer scale of the search—blinding lights, the distant wail of an ambulance, officers moving with urgent precision. The organised chaos blurred around her. She wandered aimlessly, searching for something—anything—that might anchor her to reality.

When a police officer approached, blocking her path, she tried to push past.

"But it's my son!" she cried out, her voice raw and brittle.

The officer gently, but firmly, guided her back to her brother's car. Margaret collapsed into the passenger seat, her body racked with sobs, her world unravelling as she wept into the darkness.

## Chapter 2

# The Morning after

David Black barely slept that night. The minutes dragged, heavy with dread, until the faintest hint of dawn crept over the horizon. At 5 am, driven by a gnawing anxiety, he set out for the river to search for his lost son. "At first light, I was looking for clues," David recalled later. "I thought Michael had been abducted, and I wasn't interested in looking in the river for his body. I was interested in how, why, and where. So, I was doing my own detective work."

He arrived at the town side of the bridge, his eyes scanning the ground with methodical precision. "I wanted to determine where Michael had been, where he had gone, because obviously his things were found on the other side of the river, and he would have had to have ridden his bike across. I looked everywhere on the approach to the bridge, the exit from Sturt Reserve as well, everywhere there was gravel that he might possibly have ridden along."

David retraced his son's familiar path along the river's edge, ending up at Michael's favourite fishing spot near a partly submerged weeping willow. The tree was a backdrop to countless father-son moments filled with laughter and simple lessons. The sunrise painted the sky with soft pastels, but for David, the beauty of the morning was eclipsed by a gnawing terror. "Michael, where are you, mate?" he whispered into the stillness.

A glint of plastic in the grass broke his trance. It was the lid from a bait container—the kind Michael often used to hold worms. The small discovery hit him like a punch to the gut, tethering hope and despair in equal measure.

David meticulously examined the area, searching for bike tracks, footprints, and any trace of his son. His skills as a tracker, honed in the dry, flat expanses of the Wimmera in western Victoria, served him well. "I learned how to understand how tracks are laid down and even how old they are... I can recognise the patterns."

His efforts paid off when he spotted a bike tyre's faint, raised treads—a narrow type, more like a racing bike. Nearby, he found the imprint of a BMX tyre with a distinctive flag pattern. Neither matched Michael's bike.

Later that morning, David made his way to Michael's grandmother's house, where the police had delivered his son's bike. On the way, he had picked up two friends, expert Aboriginal trackers who had volunteered to help. Michael's bike leaned against the garage wall, his canvas haversack dangling from the handlebars. David opened the bag; inside, worms wriggled alongside a lidless plastic container. When he fitted the lid he'd found near the river, it snapped on perfectly. "Michael would never leave his bag like this," David murmured, shaking his head.

With the trackers by his side, David returned to Sturt Reserve. After hours of painstaking examination, they reached a chilling consensus: there were no signs of Michael's bike tracks near the bridge.

"If Michael's things were found at Thiele Reserve, then he had to ride across the bridge. There is no other way to get there by bicycle, and I wanted to be certain that his bike had been ridden there. I checked everywhere."

The trackers were as baffled as David.

*South Australian Police Diving Squad.*

Meanwhile, specialist police divers scoured the riverbed and banks for four days, their methodical searches yielding nothing. This elite team had an impressive track record, having conducted 137 recovery operations in inland South Australian waters throughout the 1980s. Only once had they failed to recover a body—and that had been during a severe flood. Under normal conditions, a drowning victim would eventually surface. But Michael remained missing, and with each passing day, the river seemed to guard its secrets more tightly.

Two weeks after Michael went missing, a similarly aged boy drowned in the River Murray, which seemed to be a trigger for the police to downplay the disappearance as an abduction. To senior detectives, the evidence at their disposal pointed to a drowning.

Police chiefs, burdened with an overflow of pressing cases, handed the investigation over to a Murray Bridge officer, Constable Peter Tulk. In country towns like Murray Bridge, police investigations aren't just built on procedures and protocols; they rely heavily on the community's heartbeat, the whispers exchanged over fences, and the watchful eyes of neighbours who miss nothing in their own backyards.

Constable Tulk embodied the archetype of an honest country cop —a man whose integrity was woven into the town's fabric. He and his wife not only lived in Murray Bridge; they immersed themselves in its rhythms, dusty roads, and tight-knit community life. This wasn't only strategic—it was who they were. Their friendships weren't formed for personal gain, but they earned trust and honest conversations that often revealed crucial information.

Strolling down the streets of Murray Bridge, Tulk was a familiar figure, frequently hailed by residents for a friendly chat. These encounters, often starting with casual remarks about local sports, had a way of evolving into informal briefings. The townsfolk trusted him, and trust, in policing, was worth its weight in gold.

Tulk's career path had been anything but stagnant. He cut his teeth at Adelaide Police Station before heading to Port Augusta to learn a thing or two. Learn he did, but he truly came into his own in the stark, sprawling outback of Coober Pedy, 850 kilometres north of Adelaide.

The town was renowned for its dazzling opal, and its residents who sheltered from the searing summer heat in homes carved underground. In the 1970s, it was a raw, restless place—home to hard-working immigrants, displaced Aboriginal communities, and a few criminals hiding from the law. Beneath its dusty streets lay hidden fortunes. Buyers from Hong Kong, eager for the precious gem, would travel to the remote outback settlement to bargain directly with the miners, hauling in suitcases stuffed with cash—the only payment the miners would take.

Tulk thrived there, drawn to the ruggedness and the stark beauty of desert life. He and his wife stayed for four years, raising their young sons amidst the red dust and endless horizon. However, eventually, the allure of green spaces and city conveniences prevailed. The decision was sealed during a trip to Adelaide when their wide-eyed boys pleaded to stop the car so they could touch the lush parkland grass—a novelty after years surrounded by Coober Pedy's barren, lunar-like landscape.

Tulk approached Michael Black's case with the tenacity that defined his career. Leaving no stone unturned, he even conducted a time trial with a boy of Michael's age to determine how long it would take to cycle from Sturt Reserve to Thiele Reserve: twenty minutes. Meticulously piecing together witness statements, he pinpointed the last confirmed sighting of Michael as being at 2.30 pm, when he was seen speaking with a man near a Kombi Van at Sturt Reserve. The description was unsettlingly specific: a dirty white Volkswagen campervan, a man with dark hair and a bushy moustache. Another witness recalled hearing a dog's frantic barking, followed by the distinct roar of a Volkswagen speeding away from Thiele Reserve.

Refusing to let the trail go cold, Tulk reached out to the local newspaper, the Murray Valley Standard, to cast a wider net for leads. The publication ran a detailed description:

"Police are searching for a man seen talking to missing Murray Bridge boy, Michael Black, 10, on the afternoon of his disappearance. Police described the man as approximately 175 cm (5 ft 9) tall, of a thin build, well-tanned, and wearing light-coloured trousers and a shirt. The man was swimming with two children between 4 pm and 4:30 pm the day before Michael disappeared. The man was driving a white Volkswagen Kombi."

"Police are not treating the case as a kidnapping but as a disappearance."

*An identikit image of the man police sought over Michael Black's disappearance.*

The article worked. A witness, Mr Smart, stepped forward, recounting an unsettling encounter at Thiele Reserve the day before Michael vanished. A man in a white Kombi had pulled alongside him, asking, "Is there anywhere I can swim around here?" The man, with dark hair, a dark moustache, sunglasses, and possibly in his forties, made a lasting impression. When Mr Smart, walking hand-in-hand with his grandson, suggested safer spots, the man replied casually, "I like to swim in the nude."

Startled by the inappropriate remark, Smart gripped his grandson's hand tightly and walked away, his instincts on high alert.

Two local children also came forward, their stories tinged with unease. They described a man with a moustache who had played "games" with them in the water, one disturbingly dubbed "Lifesavers". He'd asked the children whether there were any special places to visit in the area, then invited them to his van if they thought of any.

Tulk's diligence had amassed a web of witness accounts, a detailed profile, and a disturbing pattern of behaviour. Yet, despite the compelling mosaic he presented, Major Crime chiefs remained unmoved. In their eyes, the case lacked sufficient evidence to warrant a higher priority. But Peter Tulk didn't need their validation. His commitment wasn't to bureaucracy but to Michael Black, justice, and a town that had trusted him with both.

# Chapter 3

# The Reluctant Witness

On the morning of January 22, 1989, the sun shone brightly through the windows of a modest house on Holly Rise, Hackham West. The air was thick with tension. Dieter Pfennig, a schoolteacher with a neatly trimmed moustache and an accent that carried faint echoes of his German roots, sat hunched at the kitchen table reading the Sunday newspaper. His strong, black coffee steamed beside an overflowing ashtray, and a cigarette dangled from his lips.

*The Sunday Mail* rustled in his hands; his dark eyes were laser-focused on what he saw.

A headline. Then a face.

The sweet face of Michael Black beamed from the newspaper. Ten years old. The kind of smile that trusted strangers. Now gone. The police were asking for anything—any sighting, any word—that could retrace the boy's last steps.

Pfennig looked over at his wife. "I saw this boy," Pfennig said quietly, his tone low and certain. The words didn't sound like a discovery. They sounded like a confession.

Sandra looked up from the table. Her eyes were weary. Their

marriage was coming apart; she'd told him she was leaving. Pfennig wasn't letting that happen without a fight.

"I saw him when I was camping," he continued. "Do you think I should go to the police?"

Sandra's mouth tightened. "Do you really have anything they don't already know?"

"There were plenty of people there," he said. "Hard to miss him—bright colours."

He muttered about not wanting to seem like an ambulance chaser. Someone sniffing around grief for attention.

The Australia Day long weekend in late January followed soon after. Despite the strained atmosphere, Pfennig suggested a family camping trip. He, Sandra, and their fifteen-year-old daughter, Petra, set off for Murray Bridge. It was meant to mark their wedding anniversary, but love was a distant memory. Pfennig claimed he wanted to show Sandra some nice spots he had discovered on a recent study trip.

They visited Sturt Reserve, where Pfennig pointed out the exact location where he claimed to have seen Michael. Later, at Thiele Reserve, on the opposite side of the river, they laid out a picnic blanket by the riverbank—mere metres from where Michael Black's bike and possessions were found. The setting was serene, but an undercurrent of unease rippled beneath the surface.

Driving onward, Pfennig crossed the bridge towards Mannum. Petra stared out the window, her mind clouded with confusion. The place her father pointed to as a fishing spot looked anything but ideal—swampy, muddy, and uninviting. She closed her eyes, exhaustion overtaking her. Petra was battling her own demons, having recently been discharged from Flinders Medical Centre after a struggle with drug and alcohol abuse.

During the Easter weekend in April, Pfennig found himself back at Sturt Reserve—this time with family and friends. He stopped at Murray Bridge for petrol, then drifted down to Sturt Reserve under the casual excuse of grabbing a snack. But this was no idle detour. He kept returning, pulled toward the same stretch of ground. Each visit felt like a quiet search for something unseen, as if the place held a secret meant only for him. The pull was invisible, but it was strong—and it was growing. Michael Black was on his mind.

Two months later, Pfennig again returned to Murray Bridge, this time canoeing with Neil C, a former student turned friend. They paddled past Sturt Reserve when Pfennig abruptly decided to stop.

"There's a toilet block there," he said casually, steering the canoe ashore.

While Pfennig disappeared into the restroom, Neil noticed a faded poster nailed to a tree—Michael Black's face staring back, a silent plea for answers. Neil pointed it out when Pfennig returned. Pfennig, unfazed, recounted where he had seen Michael and his dog, then insisted they camp there for the night.

For Dieter Pfennig, the disappearance of Michael Black was more than a passing headline. It was an obsession he couldn't seem to shake—or perhaps, one he never wanted to.

## Who is Dieter Pfennig?

Pfennig (13), along with his brother Roland (11), sister Heidi (15), and parents, arrived in Australia aboard the ship *Castel Felice*. The journey took the German family from Bremerhaven via Fremantle to Melbourne, arriving on June 29, 1961. After spending time at the Bonegilla Immigration Centre in Victoria, they were then transferred to the Woodside Immigration Centre in the Adelaide Hills, South Australia. After three weeks, they were given accommodation at a hostel in Glenelg, a popular coastal suburb of Adelaide.

Academically, Pfennig performed brilliantly through high school and went on to study at the newly opened Flinders University in the southern suburbs of Adelaide.

Pfennig was unsure of which career path to follow; he studied various subjects, including science, mathematics, philosophy, and psychiatry, and he also obtained a teaching degree. When he found himself enrolling in a Spanish course, he realised that he was delaying the inevitable; it was time for him to get a job. Pfennig began his educational career at Adelaide Boys' High, situated off West Terrace, in the Tambawadi Park, just one section of the 760 hectares of parklands surrounding the City of Adelaide. Architect Colonel William Light planned the extensive ring of parks to accommodate the "healthful recreation of the City's aspiring citizens."

The school is just minutes from the CBD and a 15-minute walk to the iconic sporting ground, Adelaide Oval. During the latter half of 1973, Pfennig left Adelaide Boys' High. There is no record of whether he was dismissed or left of his own accord.

Pfennig kept himself physically fit, albeit with a voracious smoking habit that he failed to control. He was an outstanding canoeist and, in 1988, competed in the Red Cross Marathon along the River Murray, a distance of over 400 kilometres. He worked out in various gyms and did weekly gymnastics sessions. He also coached gymnastics and volunteered at the South Coast Canoeing Club as an instructor to junior members.

Work colleagues described him as a wiz with computers and a mathematics supremo. Pfennig had an interesting and unusual combination of a love for outdoor physical activities and an analytical mind, which made him a competitive chess player. He hated losing at anything.

While at university, he met Sandra. They lived together and eventually married on January 29, 1972. Their first daughter, Petra, was born on May 15, 1973. The family lived in a unit along Henley

Beach Road, Underdale, before purchasing a new home in Hackham West in January 1977.

On most school holidays, he and his family travelled long distances to camping sites around South Australia, Broken Hill, where Sandra's parents lived, and various destinations throughout Victoria.

At the end of 1988, after 12 years at Mitchell Park High School, Pfennig quietly walked away from the familiar halls for the last time. A new position at Glengowrie High awaited him in the coming year—but his future held far darker plans than a change of scenery.

## Chapter 4

# The One That Got Away

December 30, 1989. The summer sun shone brightly on the coastal suburb of Port Noarlunga. A salty breeze drifted in from the beach, stirring the heavy stillness that had settled over the town. Most families had gone to the shoreline, leaving behind a quiet that felt deeper than usual.

Around 1:30 pm, 13-year-old Robert (not his real name) was pushing the limits of his friend's bike, soaking in the kind of carefree joy that only school holidays could offer. His sandy hair streamed behind him, tousled and dancing in the wind as he raced down the gentle slope. Robert was thirsty and was heading for the delicatessen. As he tore around the corner of Kalgoorlie Avenue and Cliff Street, his tyres screeched against the footpath, barely missing a man who stood beside a parked van.

Robert propped the bike against a shop window, beads of sweat trickling down his temples.

Just as he reached for the deli door, a voice called out. "Excuse me, could you help me here?"

The man's voice was casual and friendly, but something in its undertone made Robert pause. He turned to see Dieter Pfennig, a tall figure with a bushy black moustache and jet-black hair. His dark, sunken eyes held a glint of something Robert couldn't quite place—something unsettling.

Pfennig gestured towards the inside of his van. "My keys have fallen into a crack," he explained, raising his large hands in mock helplessness. "Look, my hands are too big."

Robert hesitated, his mother's warnings about strangers echoing faintly in his mind.

"I don't talk to strangers," he mumbled, his gaze dropping to the ground.

As Robert approached the shop door, Pfennig's smile faded, replaced by a flicker of impatience. His voice grew sharper and more insistent. "I'm in a bit of a rush; do you mind?"

Without waiting for a reply, Pfennig swung open the sliding side door, the hinges creaking in the stillness. Caught between politeness and a gnawing sense of unease, Robert stepped forward. He leaned into the van, reaching awkwardly down the side of the seat.

It happened in an instant.

Pfennig lunged, his hands like iron clamps, slamming Robert's head towards the floor. The boy barely had time to yelp before Pfennig hissed threats into his ear, promising violence if he made a sound. Efficient, practised, Pfennig bound Robert's small wrists with cord and secured duct tape over his eyes and mouth.

"Don't move, or I will punch you. You hear?" Pfennig growled.

With chilling precision, he hoisted Robert's bike into the back of the van. His eyes darted around, scanning for witnesses. But the streets remained deserted.

Satisfied, Pfennig slid into the driver's seat, an excited smile creeping across his face as he drove off, leaving nothing but the faint echo of tyres on hot asphalt and a world that would soon realise it had lost another child to a predator hiding in plain sight.

Pfennig sped off down the road. The VW motor screamed with high revs. When the boy cried out for help. Pfennig reached over and hit him. "Keep quiet or else."

Pfennig drove south along the coast for 15 minutes to Triggs Point, a popular surfing beach. He parked in a secluded area above a cliff. Pfennig lowered the tape over Robert's mouth and began perversely interrogating the frightened boy about his sexuality. Pfennig kept up a barrage of intimidating sexual statements and questions. The longer it went on, the more excited Pfennig's voice became, until it was in a state of thrill. In a horrible and perverse action, he held down the boy and masturbated over the terrified boy's bare chest. Robert began to cry.

"Please take me home, mister."

Pfennig told Robert he would set him free in the nearby sandhills, "where the death adders will get you."

Pfennig exited the vehicle, took the boy's bike out, and carefully leaned it against some shrubbery. Robert was still blindfolded but managed to peer through the bottom of the tape. What he saw looked odd. Pfennig was carefully wiping the bike clean with a cloth, as if preparing it for sale, his movements meticulous.

After leaving Robert's bike at Triggs Point, Pfennig then drove to a secluded sandy area by the river at Old Noarlunga near the old Horseshoe Inn, where he further molested the exhausted boy.

For three hours, Pfennig drove to different locations, waiting for darkness to descend so that he could safely take the boy back to his home without being seen.

Pfennig and his wife, Sandra, had separated in February 1989. Sandra and their two children no longer resided at the family home at Hackham West.

During this time, Pfennig left the boy tied up in his van while he bought a soft drink at a deli. The heat of the day was making Robert weak. Robert sucked on a straw while Pfennig chain-smoked the hours away. Pfennig questioned Robert about his parents.

"What does your father do?"

"He's retired now, living on a pension."

"Does he own his home?"

"I don't know."

Pfennig then told Michael that he was going to hold him for a ransom of $40,000.

Robert started to cry and didn't reply.

"Could he afford $10,000?"

"I don't know. Just let me go home."

Pfennig then told Robert he had an accomplice to help him get the ransom. "I need information on your parents. I will write it down."

Pfennig started peppering Robert with questions. However, the boy could see underneath his taped eyes that Pfennig had a pen and paper but was not writing anything down. Robert realised that Pfennig was playing a game with him. Robert feared he would never see his family again.

When Pfennig arrived at his Hackham West home, he kept the boy gagged with a sock in his mouth and bound in his van, waiting for total darkness. When Pfennig believed it was safe, he manoeuvred Robert into a sleeping bag and carried the boy inside. He laid Robert down in the hallway and undressed him. He then began to tie the naked boy to a wooden chair with a rope.

Pfennig offered the boy boiled carrots, but his energy was so low that he could hardly chew. He then untied the boy and carried him into the bathroom.

Only candlelight lit the room, their flames flickering against the basin's rim, casting restless shadows on the walls. Pfennig lowered the exhausted boy into the bath, the water tepid, still. With slow, measured strokes, he bathed the child with a flannel as if tending to a fragile infant, as if he were performing a ritual.

Later in the night, Pfennig gave Robert a 'choice' on how he could spend the night.

"Do you want to be tied up or would you like some pills?"

At first, the boy asked for the pills as he was fearful of being tied up all night in a sleeping bag, but quickly changed his mind as he became anxious that he would never wake up.

Pfennig was only playing mind games with the boy. He took no notice and placed one by one, four tablets down the throat of the boy. Pfennig and the boy slept in the same bed that night.

In the morning, Robert was groggy and nauseous from the pills and still numb with shock. Pfennig again tied Robert to a chair in the hallway and spoon-fed him ice cream.

Robert looked around at the walls of the passage. He stared at an image of an elephant in the centre of the wall; he then looked at the writing underneath. Printed in large letters was a house address. He thought it might be the address of where he was being held captive. He then turned his head and saw Pfennig staring at him with an evil intent. Pfennig then focused on the address on the wall. It was the address of Pfennig's home. The abductor's eyes frowned at the boy, and once again, a blindfold was applied.

At midday, Pfennig told Robert he would be gone for "ten or so minutes." A large dog was brought into the room. "If you try anything, he will eat you all up." The blindfolded boy heard the schoolteacher laughing as he walked out the front door.

Pfennig was a chronic chain smoker and had smoked his last cigarette, and he was desperate for a nicotine fix. Pfennig brazenly returned to the delicatessen where he had abducted Robert and purchased a carton of cigarettes before driving a short distance to his parents' home at Christies Beach, where he chatted with them over a cup of coffee.

Robert shook with fear as he sat naked, tied to the chair. He believed it was his last opportunity to escape certain death. He desperately tried tugging at the rope, but the harder he pulled, the tighter it seemed to become. His youthful skin was red, raw, and tender around his ankles and wrists due to the rope's tightness and abrasiveness. He then changed tack and wriggled his small fingers into the knot. His fingers were thrusting in and around the rope when he finally felt a slight loosening of the knot. Robert pulled with all his strength, and the rope slipped off his hands. He then frantically untied his legs, ripped off the silver tape from his eyes, and dislodged the sock from his mouth. Tears welled in Robert's eyes as he finally saw freedom as a real possibility.

But he suddenly froze with fright when he thought he heard a car pull up outside the house. Robert became desperate. He tried to unlock the front door but couldn't. He then ran to the back door, but again the door wouldn't budge. Robert headed for the kitchen.

He climbed onto the sink and slid the glass window to one side. He kicked with all his strength at the wire screen until it dislodged. He jumped to the ground and then scrambled over a high galvanised tin fence to a neighbour's house, and in doing so, cut his hands and legs. Robert stumbled to the front door and knocked frantically. There was no answer. He banged his fist on the door once more. Just when he thought he would have to try another house, a woman appeared. The boy pleaded with her to give him refuge. The woman was shocked at what she saw. The boy still had around his head the silver tape and the cotton wool balls dangling down over the boy's eyes; there was blood trickling from his cut, naked body.

Robert staggered into the hallway.

"Ring my daddy, please. I want my daddy." Robert collapsed on the couch, sobbing and shivering from shock.

The woman immediately grabbed a rug from her lounge and wrapped the shaking boy in it. She then called 000 and, on the police's advice, rang Robert's father.

Within minutes, three police cars screeched to a halt at Holly Rise, Hackham West. As Robert was trying to tell them about his nightmare, the familiar noise of the VW van pulled into the driveway next door. Robert ran into the arms of the neighbour, terrified. As Pfennig parked his van, police rushed towards him from every direction.

Dieter Pfennig stepped out of the van, oblivious to the storm about to descend. He didn't flinch when officers swarmed him, weapons drawn, their commands sharp and unyielding. Instead, he casually lit a cigarette, the lighter's flick incongruous with the moment's gravity. His demeanour was unsettlingly calm, almost detached.

Detective Hirlam approached Pfennig. His voice was steady but laced with restrained fury.

"We have had an allegation from a young boy that you brought him here against his will and tied him up. Is that correct?"

Pfennig exhaled a plume of smoke, his response chilling in its nonchalance.

"How did you know?" he asked, as if discussing a misplaced set of keys.

"He managed to escape while you were gone. Why did you do it?" Hirlam pressed.

Pfennig shrugged; his answer was devoid of remorse. "Loneliness. If he is in there, can you release him?"

The detective's jaw tightened. "What is your name?"

Pfennig's lips curled into a faint, unsettling smile. "Mud," he replied cryptically.

Hirlam didn't waver. "Did you have any sexual contact with him?"

Pfennig took another drag from his cigarette, then answered with terrifying simplicity. "Just fondling. I just wanted someone to hug."

The forensic team moved quickly, dismantling the Kombi Van with meticulous precision. Among the array of items they uncovered, one stood out: a large bag of lime. Its presence was ominous, a silent testament to what might have been. Lime is a substance known not only for its agricultural uses but also for its grim efficiency in hastening

*Dieter Pfennig is escorted into the Christies Beach Police Station by detectives.*

decomposition. It could strip flesh from bone, erase traces, and silence the evidence of unspeakable acts.

Was Pfennig planning to murder Robert and dispose of his body with the same calculated coldness he displayed during his confession? The answer would remain locked within the twisted corridors of Pfennig's mind. Robert had escaped, but how close did he come to becoming another unsolved mystery? This was a question that haunted everyone who touched the case. The thin line between life and death had never felt more fragile.

Pfennig was taken to the Christies Beach Police Station and charged with abduction and a string of sexual offences. The TV stations immediately pounced on the sensational story and broadcast

Pfennig's occupation and suburb of residence, but obviously not his name.

Pfennig was allowed to make a phone call to organise legal representation. He phoned his wife, Sandra.

"I've been arrested; can you find me a solicitor?"

"What do you mean? Arrested for what?"

"Kidnapping and sexual assault."

"Kidnapping!"

"Yes, a boy."

Sandra's mouth went instantly dry. She was stunned. All she could reply with was a bland, "I'll see what I can do."

At the time, Sandra was a coordinator in a community legal service. She believed her husband had called only to see if she had any legal contacts who could come out on New Year's Eve, so she refused to make any calls.

Pfennig phoned her a few hours later. "Any luck with a solicitor?"

"No." Sandra could barely contain her rage and demanded that her husband tell her what had happened. "What did you do, go out in the streets and just pick somebody off the streets?"

"Yes."

"Why did you do it?"

"Well, I was lonely… and I have been thinking of it on and off for the past 12 months."

"Did you tie them up?"

"Yes."

Sandra couldn't believe her husband's insipid answers. "Look, you know this just is not acceptable; loneliness is not an acceptable excuse."

She then asked Pfennig about other incidents involving boys she knew that Pfennig had been accused of in the past. "Are they, therefore, true?"

"Not exactly."

"What do you mean by that?"

"No, no, none of that was true."

Exasperated, Sandra asked Pfennig what exactly happened.

"I just grabbed him and threw him into the van; I picked someone up at random."

Sandra said, "I told you that you needed help."

Pfennig's voice shrank to a whisper. "I think I am crying out for help. This is part of what I am doing."

The other accusations against Pfennig involved two separate instances of alleged child molestation. There was an incident involving a complaint by a boy who lived nearby, around 1983–84.

Sandra said, "He took the boy on a fishing trip, and there was fondling going on. You show me yours, and I will show you mine type of incident."

The other incident involved a male student of Pfennig's.

Sandra said, "Both of them were involved in a chess club. He came frequently to our house to play chess."

Pfennig was never charged with any criminal offence from these allegations.

Living with Pfennig was at times awkward to say the least. Pfennig had admitted to Sandra to having had sex with men on a number of occasions before their marriage. Pfennig had revealed to Sandra a sexual encounter when he was at an Army camp.

"He talked about some incident that had occurred at an Army camp with one or more males, and that he introduced me later to one of the men involved. The army camp was around 1969–70; it was a Christmas camp."

Sandra said, "He got drunk one night and had sexual activity with a number of other males, two or three, I think. He indicated he thought he might have been raped and that there was oral activity—oral sex. I think he was intrigued and curious about the experience."

At one time, Pfennig even invited one of the young army men around to their home. It was planned to be more than a social encounter.

Sandra said, "He arranged a meeting for the man to come to our house. I understood that there was to be sex between the two of them, and I was to go out for the evening or simply not be in that part of the house. The man, he did not come because some other people came to the house, and we were having a bit of a party, and he didn't come over."

Pfennig's conversations with his wife after his release were insightful.

Pfennig: "I have been thinking of it on and off for the past 12 months."

This admission that he had been thinking of abducting a child for a year ties in with the timeline of the disappearance of Michael Black. It also suggested that Pfennig was having constant fantasies of child abduction.

Sandra: "Did you tie them up?"

Pfennig: "I think I am crying out for help. This is part of what I am doing."

Could Pfennig be telling the truth? Did he want to end his child sexual cravings by being incarcerated?

## Chapter 5

# Similar Facts

The night Pfennig was arrested for the abduction of Robert, a sergeant at Christies Beach Police Station received a phone call from a woman. She wanted to know if they had Dieter Pfennig in custody.

"Yes, we have."

"Is it to do with the abduction of the boy from Port Noarlunga?"

"In relation to an alleged abduction, yes."

"Well, I probably need to talk to a detective."

The arresting officers drove to the nearby suburb to take a statement. They immediately phoned Major Crime.

The caller provided information regarding the disappearance of Michael Black. The informer told police that Pfennig had visited her home shortly after Black's disappearance. She claimed Pfennig and several other friends were watching television when a report on the search for Black appeared.

Pfennig told them that he was at Sturt Reserve that day and had spoken to the missing boy. The informer recalled that the room went silent with this incredible admission.

When Sandra Pfennig was interviewed regarding Michael Black's disappearance, she stated that her husband had left home on January 15 in his white Kombi Van and returned home on January 20. He had told her a story about how he needed time out to study for his new teaching position. Pfennig's van was like a home away from home, with a television, radio, cooking facilities, and sleeping accommodation.

In 1990, Pfennig pleaded guilty to having abducted and raped Robert at Port Noarlunga. He was sentenced to 15 years in prison.

Detective Lyn Strange, who headed the investigation, believed there were too many similarities between how Robert's bicycle had been left at the beach and how Michael Black's bicycle and clothing had been left at Murray Bridge. He believed there was a pattern of criminal behaviour that police could pursue.

Because of the publicity in the media regarding the sentencing of Pfennig, police began receiving information about the disgraced high-school teacher. In custody, Pfennig was questioned about Michael Black. He admitted to seeing Michael at Sturt Reserve but denied going to Thiele Reserve on 18 January. Police eventually accumulated several witnesses who saw Pfennig's distinctive Kombi Van at Thiele Reserve the afternoon of the abduction. Police charged Pfennig with the abduction and murder of Michael Black, believing that they now had enough evidence for a conviction.

The night Michael went missing, the entire search was focused on Thiele Reserve, which was understandable, as that is where Michael's belongings were found. However, good basic police work rightfully turned the focus of the abduction back towards Sturt Reserve, where Michael had always planned to fish.

A witness claimed she heard a commotion on January 18 at

Thiele Reserve. Mrs Gould and her husband lived in a home which overlooked the northern end of Thiele Reserve. It has a large deck that provides extensive views of the Murray and parts of the reserve. Around 3 pm, she heard a vehicle come into the reserve. She then listened to what she described as a commotion associated with that vehicle. There was a loud revving of the engine, followed by the noise of tyres spinning on gravel. She then heard a door slam shut, followed by the loud barking of a dog. What she particularly took note of was that the barking continued after the vehicle drove away. The observant woman also recalled that the vehicle had a noticeable rattle to the engine noise.

Over a year after Michael Black disappeared, police took several vehicles to Thiele Reserve, drove them into the reserve, and asked Mrs Gould to listen to the noise of each vehicle. A police officer drove in, paused by the toilet block, slammed the vehicle's door, and drove away. Mrs Gould couldn't see any of these vehicles, relying only on her hearing. The police used eight vehicles, including Pfennig's Volkswagen Kombi Van and another Kombi Van. Pfennig's van was driven through twice in positions four and nine.

Mrs Gould nominated numbers four and nine as making the noise she thought was most like that she had heard on 18 January 1989.

## Chapter 6

# Pfennig v Crown

The trial of Dieter Pfennig was destined to be controversial from the start. Securing a murder conviction without a body was a rare feat, but the Crown prosecutors had a powerful weapon in their arsenal—one that could make or break the case. They intended to introduce evidence of Pfennig's prior conviction for the abduction and rape of a 13-year-old boy at Port Noarlunga, known in this trial only as "H". That attack had occurred only eleven months after Michael Black vanished from Sturt Reserve.

Typically, a defendant's past crimes are kept hidden from jurors, as they are deemed too prejudicial to be admitted in court. But this time, the prosecution argued that Pfennig's actions against H weren't just history—they were critical to establishing a disturbing pattern. They pursued a conviction based on "similar fact" evidence, supported by damning testimony from fellow inmates who claimed Pfennig had made chilling admissions behind bars.

Justice Cox, the trial judge, conducted a rigorous *voir dire*, a pre-trial hearing to decide whether H's evidence would be admissible. After weighing the arguments, he ruled that it would be. The reasoning was stark and unsettling: Pfennig had been at Sturt Reserve when Michael Black disappeared. He owned a vehicle large enough to transport the boy, his dog, his bicycle, and his fishing gear. And crucially, he had admitted to speaking with Michael that day.

Justice Cox went further. He determined that Pfennig's prior attack on H exposed a disturbing propensity—a willingness to target young boys, to lure them, and to act on his violent impulses. The similarities between the two cases were too striking to ignore. On this basis, the judge allowed the evidence to be heard, setting the stage for a courtroom battle that would be as contentious as it was heartbreaking.

Justice Cox told the court that drowning was not a reasonable explanation for Michael's disappearance because of the improbability that the boy went to the Thiele Reserve when he was known to dislike the place, he was not noticed by anyone there, and no body was found despite extensive searching of the river. Cox explained to the court that the only rational alternative to drowning was abduction, which Pfennig's counsel condoned.

Witness H, who was now 15 years of age, bravely described to the court how Pfennig bound and gagged him after asking him to retrieve keys from inside Pfennig's Volkswagen van. The boy said Pfennig sexually abused him several times during a 24-hour period.

Asked if he could recognise the man who abducted him, the boy said "yes" and nervously pointed towards Pfennig sitting in the dock.

### "... just felt like doing a good deed"

Pfennig took the stand with a veneer of confidence, his posture steady as he settled into the witness box. His demeanour suggested a man prepared, perhaps rehearsed, with each gesture measured and each glance seemingly calculated to convey credibility.

Under direct questioning, Pfennig acknowledged his presence at Sturt Reserve on January 18. He recounted his reasoning with casual clarity, painting a picture of a man seeking solitude before embarking on a new teaching position. According to him, it was a simple, reflective getaway in his VW Kombi Van—an escape beginning from his Hackham West home on January 15, with stops at various camping sites including Brownhill Creek at Mitcham, Rapid Bay, and ultimately, Sturt Reserve in Murray Bridge.

Pfennig: "I had what I sometimes refer to as a 'Japanese bladder', so I need to go to the toilet probably more often than most people. And I parked right opposite where the toilets are," he explained, his words delivered with an air of offhanded honesty, as if such mundane details were beyond reproach.

Pfennig seemed to anticipate every query, offering explanations as if they'd been rehearsed in front of a mirror. When asked about his choice of campsite, he leaned on sentimentality.

"I found this to be a very nice spot and in particular the Bunyip was something that was new to me and I know that my younger daughter was reading, I think at the time, Enid Blyton stories, in which there was a bunyip, and I thought this is something I have got to tell her about when I get back."

The Bunyip was a mechanical creature designed to enthral tourists along the Murray River. It emerged from murky waters when coins were deposited, an odd, almost surreal detail juxtaposed against the grim undertone of the trial.

Witnesses had observed Pfennig at the local kiosk, engaging with children. He recounted this interaction with a self-effacing charm:

"While I was waiting, there were some children, four or five, working out on their fingers what they could afford with the money that they had and working out whether everybody got their fair share – so on – and as a maths teacher, that sort of thing makes maths worthwhile. So, I was enjoying myself watching that. I think they had about three or four attempts – each time a few cents short – and when they got within three cents, I said, well, I would pay the difference to the attendant. I was told you shouldn't do that. I said, 'but I want to – just felt like doing a good deed.'"

Pfennig's narrative was rich with seemingly innocuous detail, and he painted himself as the benevolent teacher, the attentive father, and the benign camper.

When pressed about his first sighting of Michael Black, his recollection was vivid:

"I was on the blanket in front of the van studying. There is a small retaining wall just there, and I was sort of sitting or leaning against that – with a blanket – I mean, my sleeping bag was rolled up."

He described watching Michael catch a fish.

"European carp – reasonable size and he was trying to beat it to death with the edge of a thong."

Pfennig recounted, "I yelled across, Hey, haven't you got a knife?"

Michael replied, "No."

"I said, Hang on. I'll get you one. I went to the van, got one of the knives out of the van, and went over and showed him how to dispatch a fish."

Pfennig's account continued:

"I did notice shortly after, and again I cannot tell you the exact duration of time, that he had walked over to where the rubbish bin was, and he was giving the fish a ceremonial burial. I am not sure whether he was singing out the Last Post; he was certainly saluting the fish as he put it in the rubbish bin."

He claimed Michael returned the knife promptly.

"I said, just put it in the back of the van. The van's door was open. It was getting hot at that stage, that's why I had moved to the outside rather than continuing working inside. When he came back, he said, 'You have got a TV inside.' I left the TV on. I generally work with background noise rather than – I cannot work in absolute silence."

Pfennig added, "I asked him whether the cricket was on. He went back to the van to have a look, stayed there for a while to have a look."

As if chronicling a mundane day, he described packing up shortly thereafter and heading into town.

When questioned about the exact time of his departure from Sturt Reserve, his answer wavered with calculated uncertainty:

"That would be close to the latest time. I believe that I left earlier than that. I now think it was between 2:15 and 2:30. I would have left before 2.30. It could have been 2.45, but it is unlikely to have been as late as that. It is unlikely that I left via Sturt Reserve Road, but I can't exclude that."

Pfennig firmly denied visiting Thiele Reserve on January 18.

After leaving Sturt Reserve, he claimed to have stopped at a butcher's shop on Murray Bridge's main street, later driving down a dead-end road where he spoke to an unidentified farmer. The farmer remained elusive, never identified or located. From there, Pfennig detailed his travels through several towns, camping in his van each night before returning home on January 20.

His testimony, dense with specifics, left an impression: whether of meticulous truth or carefully curated fiction, it was for the jury to decide.

## "I wasn't in charge of my actions"

Pfennig was later questioned about what motivated him to abduct and rape H, the Port Noarlunga boy. His response was unsettling in its detached introspection:

"I have asked myself the question why I did this many times – as I stated for the last two years – for something like the first 8 months, I couldn't see beyond the fact that I was extremely exhausted, tired, my mind was fuzzy, I had just fallen asleep in the sun, and everything was like a dream. I mean, I wasn't in charge of my actions. Things happened. I didn't plan anything. I didn't say, 'Well, I'll do that, and I will do that.' It was just like a dream. Events just happened, and you are not in charge of it."

The courtroom remained tense, each word hanging heavily in the air, the gravity of his admission stark against his casual delivery.

When asked why he placed the boy's bike in his van, Pfennig responded with an eerie simplicity:

"Well, after I finished tying him up, I shut the door, and then the bike was still there on the footpath. I mean, if the shoes had been there, I would have put them in, too. It just seemed to be one and the same thing. He was there, the bike was his, and they just went together... It was just that the two went together. You couldn't take one without the other."

His words, devoid of remorse, painted a chilling portrait of a man describing not crimes, but mundane tasks. The jury listened, the weight of his testimony settling like a shadow over the proceedings.

**Prisoner Evidence**

Bringing forward evidence from fellow prisoners in a murder trial is fraught with peril, a double-edged sword capable of cutting both ways. The courtroom had seen it before. In 1983, during the trial concerning the death of Louise Bell, Raymond John Geesing was convicted mainly on the testimony of fellow inmates. That conviction, built on a fragile foundation of prison-yard whispers and dubious claims, crumbled on appeal when it was revealed there was no concrete evidence linking him to the crime. The stark reality: fellow prisoners had fabricated statements that stitched Geesing into a narrative he did not belong to.

A decade later, echoes of that case reverberated through the courtroom as prisoner testimony surfaced again, this time against Pfennig.

A prisoner named Sutton took the stand. His demeanour was self-assured. Sutton claimed that Pfennig had confided in him, sharing chilling details with the casualness of a man recounting an everyday errand.

"(Pfennig) had told me he had talked to the boy and became friendly with him," Sutton testified, his voice steady.

According to Sutton, Pfennig described how he had lured the boy with the promise of new fishing equipment stashed in his van.

"Raised the boy's interest in some new fishing equipment which was in his van, and took him back to the van and showed the fishing equipment to him. Once the boy was in the van, he said that he had grabbed the boy, pushed him to the floor... that he had used tape to bind his hands and feet and gag him, and he put all the boy's belongings beside the river."

Sutton went further, claiming Pfennig admitted to taking the boy home and holding him captive. On the surface, this detail strained credulity—Pfennig's wife was living with him at the time, present in the home. But could "home" have meant somewhere else? Perhaps his parents' residence on Clovelly Avenue, Christies Beach? It is only five kilometres from his home in Hackham West. Pfennig had grown up there. His retired parents often travelled with their caravan, leaving the house vacant except for Pfennig's sporadic visits to tend the garden and collect the mail.

Then came the most harrowing part of Sutton's testimony:

"(Pfennig) had raped the boy orally and anally and eventually bashed and choked the boy to death after the boy had bitten him on his penis, and that he had waited until night-time to bury the body at a place near Kingston-on-Murray."

Sutton claimed Pfennig even provided directions to the burial site. Acting on this, police conducted extensive digs in the area. The earth yielded no answers—no trace of Michael Black's body.

But Sutton was not the only inmate to come forward. Testimony from three other prisoners painted a similarly dark picture. One of them, an enigmatic figure known in Adelaide's entertainment circles as 'Rose-Royal,' claimed to have documented conversations with Pfennig, scribbled in an elaborate, almost theatrical code.

Among Rose-Royal's cryptic notes:

- "He was able to gain children's trust easily."
- "He had killed at least three people."
- "Dabbles in the occult."

Rose-Royal's testimony grew stranger still. He described observing

Pfennig's peculiar fixation with a particular prison library book, "The Summoning." According to Rose-Royal, Pfennig borrowed it repeatedly, often scribbling notes in the margins. Curious, Rose-Royal claimed he inspected the book, finding numerous underlined passages.

Highlighted phrases included:
- "Stealth and cunning, these were the watchwords of the order."
- "The order was select, and there was great safety in keeping their numbers small. They also needed a ready supply of mortals to sacrifice on the altar of their longevity."
- "Children were irrelevant to them of the order, save when they could be used as instruments to the order's own ends."

The courtroom absorbed these words with a mixture of horror and scepticism. Were these revelations the truth? Or were they elaborate fabrications, crafted by men with murky motives?

In the end, the jury would have to decide: Was this damning testimony genuine, or another tale spun in prison, where truth and manipulation often shared the same cell?

The prosecution produced dozens of witnesses, giving the court a definitive timeline for Michael Black's and Pfennig's whereabouts.

## January 17, 1989

At around 4:00 pm, a witness, Mr Smart, recalled an unsettling encounter. He testified that Pfennig approached him, his demeanour casual yet with an undercurrent of something less benign, asking if he knew of any places suitable for nude swimming. Mr Smart, unsuspecting of any sinister motive, directed him to Thiele Reserve.

Shortly thereafter, the court heard, Pfennig was seen mingling with two children swimming from the Sturt Reserve wharf. In an almost rehearsed, friendly manner, he inquired about interesting local spots and casually extended an invitation to join him in his van. Fortunately, the children declined, and their instincts or perhaps just sheer luck kept them from potential danger.

**January 18, 1989**

**1:30 pm** — Michael Black left his father's home, pedalling towards Sturt Reserve on his bicycle, which would have taken him about ten minutes.

**1:55 pm** — Mr Haines, a key witness, first spotted Michael at Sturt Reserve.

**2:00 pm** — Michael visited the river kiosk, served by Miss Giles and Mrs Regnier, both of whom knew him well. Miss Giles testified that she observed Michael on three separate occasions beginning at approximately 2:00 pm, with the first two visits occurring at twenty-minute intervals and the third about thirty minutes after the second. Michael purchased chips and an ice cream. She placed the final interaction close to 3:00 pm.

Mrs Regnier was primarily occupied with cooking but recalled serving Michael once, which she estimated to be around 2:00 pm. In her initial statements and during her committal testimony, Mrs Regnier indicated that she remembered seeing Michael at the latest by 3:00 pm.

**2:25 pm** — Mr Haines again observed Michael, this time conversing with a man fitting Pfennig's description: around 5'10" to 5'11", light build, clear complexion, dark brown hair, and about 40 years old. The only inconsistency was the absence of facial hair in Haines' description, while Pfennig sported a moustache. Notably, despite having lived in Murray Bridge for 25 years, Haines did not recognise the man.

**2:45 pm** — Mr Toogood, a council employee, witnessed an old white Kombi Van speeding unsafely away from Sturt Reserve towards Murray Bridge's main street, a route leading towards Thiele Reserve. Earlier, Toogood had noticed a similar van heading towards Sturt Reserve.

**3:00-3:30 pm** — Mrs Gould, whose home overlooked Thiele Reserve, testified to hearing a commotion below her house. The prosecution put forward that this noise was Pfennig's van, potentially with an incapacitated Michael inside. They theorised that Pfennig's purpose for visiting Thiele Reserve was to plant Michael's dog, Bessie, and his belongings to fabricate a drowning scenario, diverting suspicion from Sturt Reserve, where Pfennig had been conspicuously present. In an experiment, Mrs Gould identified the noise she heard as similar to Pfennig's van. Around 3:20 pm, Michael's dog was seen nearby.

**3:25 pm** — A witness named Bernardi noticed Michael's bicycle leaning against the railing near Thiele Reserve's toilet block.

**4:00 pm** — Mr Jones, who went water-skiing at Thiele Reserve, testified to seeing a Kombi Van parked off-road opposite the boat ramp, in proximity to where Michael's bicycle and belongings were later found. His description matched Pfennig's van.

Michael was never seen at Sturt Reserve again after Mr. Toogood sighted the van around 2:45 pm, a detail the prosecution underscored. Many people who knew Michael were present at the Reserve, yet none saw him after that time.

Adding to the weight of evidence, Pfennig's daughter, Petra, testified about her father's interactions with Michael at Sturt Reserve.

She recounted her father admitting he had spoken to Michael and patted his dog. Petra stated that Pfennig mentioned seeing Michael twice that day, a claim he later dismissed, suggesting she must have misunderstood.

The prosecution painted a compelling timeline: Pfennig was at Sturt Reserve with Michael, conversing with him, and near his van. He left the Reserve around the time Michael vanished. Mrs Gould's testimony linked Pfennig's van to Thiele Reserve, where Michael's belongings were found. Crucially, Pfennig's account of his movements post-Sturt Reserve lacked corroboration, leaving a trail of unanswered questions and growing suspicions.

The trial judge, after hearing the evidence of almost 100 witnesses, made certain specific findings:

"It would, in my opinion, be an affront to common sense to postulate two persons in Michael Black's vicinity at Murray Bridge, and both almost certainly at Sturt Reserve, about the same time that afternoon, each with a propensity to kidnap and sexually assault young boys and each having the physical means that afternoon of doing so, one of them befriending the boy and lending him a fishing knife and the other within a fairly short space of time but quite independently engaging, presumably, in some kind of pre-abduction dealing with him, however brief, and both leaving Sturt Reserve in separate vehicles at much the same time."

Cox pointed to the similarities in the pattern of conduct which must have been engaged in by Michael's abductor and by Pfennig in the H incident, particularly leaving the victim's belongings in a way that was calculated to lay a false trail and suggest accidental drowning—compare the disposal of H's bicycle at Port Noarlunga. However, Justice Cox noted that the fact that there was no murder in the case of H was a significant dissimilarity which would usually tell against the admission of the H evidence. But the inconclusiveness of the evidence as to Pfennig's intentions concerning the ultimate fate of the boy militated against that treatment of it.

Cox thought the two crimes' fundamental similarity, including Pfennig's behaviour at Sturt Reserve and laying a false trail with the bicycle, gave them an "underlying unity".

After deliberating for only 24 hours, the jury returned to a courtroom thick with tension and anticipation.

Justice Cox's voice was steady as he addressed the foreman. "Have you reached a unanimous verdict?"

The reply was swift: "We have, Your Honour."

The foreman stood, the weight of his words pressing down on the silent crowd. "Guilty of murder," he announced. The courtroom exhaled collectively—an audible sigh rippled through the space.

Michael Black's mother, seated with fragile dignity, succumbed to quiet tears, her grief momentarily unguarded.

In the dock, Dieter Pfennig was a statue—impassive, motionless. No flicker of emotion crossed his face, no sign of the verdict's impact. The police officers who had tirelessly pursued justice allowed themselves a fleeting sense of satisfaction, though their work felt incomplete. The haunting question remained: Where was Michael Black's body?

Determined, investigators turned their focus to Pfennig's home. They tore through it with relentless precision, ripping up floorboards and excavating the Hackham West backyard with heavy machinery.

Yet the ground held its secrets tight. The search yielded nothing, and Michael's resting place remained elusive.

Unwilling to give up, Detectives Alan Arthur and Lyn Strange visited Pfennig in his Yatala Prison cell. They hoped to coax the truth from him, to appeal to any shard of conscience he might possess. But Pfennig was resolute. "I didn't do it," he claimed, dismissing the evidence as a setup. His denial was as cold and unyielding as his demeanour in court.

Outside the courtroom, David Black faced the media with remarkable composure. "I am not bitter," he began, his voice steady despite the storm of emotion beneath. "I am grateful for having had Michael for 10 years. I am a forgiving person, but I don't understand why Dieter Pfennig appeared and why he did this to Michael. I always knew what happened to Michael. I knew he did not drown; I have always known."

David Black's gratitude extended to the jury. "They knew what was going on. It would be horrible to pass a guilty verdict, but they got it right. After all that time, it's pretty amazing. We are all still healing, and this—this court case—is just part of it."

He also praised the detectives of the Major Crime Task Force. "They have done a marvellous job, and I think they go a little unnoticed sometimes."

Michael's mother, her voice fragile but filled with relief, echoed his sentiments. "As you can imagine, it has been very stressful. I want to thank the Major Crime Squad for the effort they have put into this case. It's been a hard job for them, and I am very appreciative."

Standing outside the courthouse, Detective Sergeant Lyn Strange, flanked by his colleagues, shared his reflections. "It's a sense of relief," he admitted. "It's been a long, arduous investigation for over two years. Certainly, a difficult investigation and one that you wouldn't want to go through too often."

Strange revealed that this was one of the two most complex cases of his career—the other being the disappearance of 10-year-old Louise Bell from her Hackham West home in early 1983. Yet, despite the verdict, he emphasised, "The file on Michael Black will remain open as his body has yet to be found. We would certainly go to any lengths to try and recover the body."

The search for Michael Black's final resting place continued—a relentless pursuit of the truth, undeterred by time, fuelled by love, and driven by the unyielding need for closure.

## Justice Upheld

Dieter Pfennig had tried to argue that his conviction was unfair. The jury should never have heard about what he did to another boy, only a year after Michael Black disappeared. However, the High Court dismissed his appeal, rejecting his claims and upholding the verdict that led to his imprisonment.

The case against Pfennig for Michael's 1989 murder had always been circumstantial—no body, no eyewitnesses. The 10-year-old had vanished from Murray Bridge, and despite exhaustive searches, his remains were never found. But authorities had ruled out accidental drowning, and the evidence pointed in one chilling direction: Pfennig.

The trial judge made a pivotal decision—to allow the jury to hear about another crime Pfennig had committed a year later. A 13-year-old boy; abducted and raped. The judge saw a disturbing pattern, an "underlying unity" between the two cases.

In a unanimous ruling in Pfennig's appeal, the High Court justices determined that this so-called "similar fact" evidence was not only relevant but essential. Such evidence, they stated, was admissible when it revealed striking similarities, an unmistakable pattern, when common sense left no room for coincidence.

In the context of Michael Black's disappearance, the judges found, the latter abduction and rape proved more than just a history of criminal behaviour. It demonstrated Pfennig's intent and method. It showed exactly who he was.

And, most importantly, it left no reasonable doubt.

There was only one explanation for Michael Black's disappearance— the one the prosecution had argued all along.

Pfennig was guilty. And now, there was no escaping it.

\* \* \*

**An Afterthought**

In 2015, I sat down with retired Detective Sergeant Lyn Strange at a quiet hotel bar in the northern suburbs of Adelaide. Even after all these years, his disdain for Dieter Pfennig was unmistakable. It wasn't the kind of professional disgust a cop feels for a criminal—it ran deeper than that.

Strange had retired from the force some years earlier, throwing himself into a new career in building construction. He earned his builder's licence, built his home, and stayed relentlessly busy. That was the kind of man he was—disciplined, methodical, unwilling to leave a job unfinished. However, the case of Michael Black was different. It was the one case he could never put to rest.

He told me about the heartbreak the case had caused the Black family. They had got their conviction, but justice felt incomplete. The missing boy's remains were still out there, and it haunted them. It haunted him, too. Cases like this—the abduction and murder of a child—weren't just rare; they were the kind that left permanent scars on the men and women who investigated them.

Strange had spent hours trying to get Pfennig to talk, to reveal where Michael's body was. He tried reasoning with him, appealing to whatever shred of humanity might be left in him.

"Think about what this would mean to his parents," he had said. "To let them say goodbye to their son."

But Pfennig's response was always the same. A blank look. Sometimes, a smirk. He wasn't the killer, he insisted, over and over again. He said it with a detachment that made Strange's blood boil.

"He was so blasé about the whole thing," Strange told me, his jaw tightening at the memory. "It was like he enjoyed the pain he was causing the Black family just by keeping silent."

For a man as disciplined as Strange, it was one of the few times he had ever felt his patience truly tested.

And yet, even after all these years, the mystery remained. Pfennig had stolen Michael Black's life. And even in silence, he still held him hostage.

# PART 3
# Cold Case Review

## Chapter 1

# Justice for Louise

The disappearance of Louise Bell stands as a haunting reminder that time does not erase the need for justice. Decades may pass, but for law enforcement officers and victims' families, a case such as Louise's is never shelved—it simply waits for the right moment, the right technological advancement, or the right person to step forward with the missing piece of the puzzle.

In South Australia, the officers of SAPOL's Cold Case Homicide team refuse to let unsolved cases slip into the shadows. To them, a murder case is never abandoned to gather dust on some forgotten shelf. Justice delayed is not justice denied—it is merely justice in waiting.

A serious crime investigation in Australia is classified as a cold case if it remains unsolved for over 12 months with no arrest in sight. Yet, unsolved does not mean ignored. SAPOL follows a meticulous, structured approach to revisiting these cases, ensuring that no lead, piece of evidence, or tip is left unexamined.

When a cold case, such as Louise's abduction, is reviewed, every detail of the case is comprehensively examined. Every element of the investigation—every statement, every forensic sample, every exhibit—is scrutinised with fresh eyes. Detectives compile detailed reports highlighting new angles, discrepancies, or potential breakthroughs.

These reports are then presented to SAPOL's Cold Case Homicide Evaluation Committee, a team of seasoned investigators who decide on the next course of action. Should resources be allocated to a renewed pursuit? Is there enough to reopen the case and bring it back into the public's focus? Each case receives careful, measured attention, ensuring that the pursuit of justice never falters.

Forensic science, the ever-evolving ally of investigators, offers new hope where once there was none. Advances in DNA analysis enable police to extract profiles from samples that were once considered too small to be useful. Perhaps the most ground-breaking tool in a detective's arsenal today would have seemed unimaginable decades ago: the rise of ancestry websites and consumer DNA databases. A single strand of DNA, a forgotten fleck of genetic material, can now be the key to unlocking the past. By working alongside forensic genealogists, SAPOL can trace unknown suspects through family connections, unmasking criminals who once believed they had escaped justice. Genetic genealogy has revolutionised the hunt for killers, linking crime scene DNA to distant relatives of unknown suspects—a technique that has proved instrumental in identifying killers worldwide.

Digital advancements also offer new possibilities, such as enhancing grainy surveillance footage, pinpointing locations through revisited phone records, and uncovering long-overlooked digital breadcrumbs.

Yet, some of the most crucial breakthroughs come not from forensic science, but from people. Time changes relationships, and fear that once silenced witnesses may no longer hold them captive. Someone afraid to speak may now find the courage to come forward. SAPOL actively seeks these voices, launching public awareness campaigns and re-interviewing individuals whose memories, perspectives, or circumstances may have shifted over the years. Psychological research confirms what experienced detectives have always known—memory is not static. It changes, deepens, sharpens, and sometimes, it reveals the truth when the moment is right.

For those who pursued Louise Bell's killer, giving up was never an option. They followed the trail for years, refusing to let time erase her name from their case files. It was not only about solving a crime—it was about restoring dignity, bringing closure to a grieving family, and proving that justice, no matter how long delayed, would always be served.

## Police dig for Louise's remains

July 2012 — The start of the breakthrough in Louise Bell's disappearance came nearly thirty years after she vanished without a trace. Now, with the aid of new forensic technology, police turned their attention once again to the backyard of convicted child killer Dieter Pfennig.

Pfennig, already behind bars for the murder of Michael Black, had long been a suspect in Louise's abduction. Major Crime Squad detectives and forensic experts descended upon Pfennig's former home in Holly Rise, Hackham West, determined to uncover the truth.

The search began under ominous conditions—relentless rain and howling southerly winds made the excavation all the more gruelling. Yet the investigators pressed on, determined to find what had been buried for so long.

The case had been reopened the previous year to take advantage of cutting-edge forensic advancements in DNA profiling.

The police enlisted the Australian Federal Police, utilising ground-penetrating radar capable of detecting anomalies beneath concrete, hoping the latest technology would provide them with the key they had been missing.

Detectives had previously targeted Pfennig's home in 1991. They pulled up floorboards and excavated a section of the yard then, but now, with new tools at their disposal, they aimed to be more precise.

Superintendent Moyle addressed the media.

"Hopefully, we can unravel some more evidence and bring some closure to the family," he said.

"In 1991, they used an excavator to dig through layers of soil, but now we can use radar to pinpoint specific areas. That allows us to focus our excavation where the ground shows disturbances."

He was careful, however, not to offer false hope.

"While current forensic testing initially appears encouraging, I don't want to raise the hopes of Louise's family unnecessarily."

Despite painstaking efforts to sieve through every grain of dirt for evidence, three days of extensive digging yielded nothing definitively linked Pfennig to the crime.

Then, at last, came an arrest.

November 2013 — A man appeared briefly in court, charged with the 1983 murder of Louise Bell. South Australian police took him into custody at Port Lincoln. The man accused was none other than Dieter Pfennig. Now 65, he appeared via video link and was remanded in custody until a later court date.

Deputy Commissioner Grant Stevens acknowledged the heartbreaking passage of time but praised the unrelenting work of detectives and forensic experts.

"This arrest is the result of years of dedication by both police and Forensic Science SA," he said. "Louise's family has endured three decades of anguish. They remain hopeful that her remains will one day be found."

A $200,000 reward had been offered for information leading to an arrest, but science ultimately delivered the long-awaited breakthrough.

The case had gripped Adelaide for decades, much like the infamous disappearance of the Beaumont children in 1966. South Australia's most respected investigative reporter, Nigel Hunt, who had followed the case from its inception, reflected on its impact.

"This was one of those cases that changed the psyche of Adelaide," he said. "A young girl taken from the sanctuary of her own bedroom—it shook the city just as the Beaumont case did."

Still, a conviction would not be easy.

"Proving guilt beyond a reasonable doubt after thirty years presents challenges," Hunt warned. "Memories fade, witnesses disappear. It will be a difficult case."

For now, though, there was progress.

Commissioner Stevens assured the public that despite the arrest, the search for Louise's body would continue.

"We never close the book," he said. "We keep investigating. We understand the trauma these families go through. We encourage them to maintain hope."

It was not yet closure for the Bell family, but it was a step closer to justice.

## Chapter 2

# Pfennig Back in Court

September 2015 — Dieter Pfennig's defence counsel decided that trial by judge alone instead of a jury was their best option for an acquittal. It was a gamble, but one Dieter Pfennig's defence team believed was worth taking—a trial by judge alone, no jury to sway, no emotional undercurrents to navigate. Just one man, Justice Michael David, would decide his fate. Given the overwhelming media coverage labelling Pfennig as a convicted child killer following his trial for Michael Black's murder, it seemed like the safest option. The public was already well aware of his violent past. Simply put, the chances of securing a fair trial were slim, regardless of how disciplined the jurors were. No matter how often they were instructed to focus solely on the evidence, their subconscious bias against a convicted child murderer would inevitably influence their judgment.

Justice Michael David came out of retirement to take on the case. David had enjoyed a wide-ranging career as both a prosecutor and a defence lawyer. He had been involved with some of the most notorious criminal cases in South Australia's legal history. David was the defence lawyer for Henry Keogh, who was found guilty of murdering his fiancée in a bath in 1994, before having his conviction quashed in 2014. He prosecuted disgraced high-ranking cop Barry Moyse, who was at the time head of the S.A. Police Drug Squad by day and at night morphed into a major player in Adelaide's drug trade. He also defended SA Police officers in the infamous Dr George Duncan drowning in the River Torrens, where plain-clothed Vice Squad members were accused of throwing the homosexual academic into the River Torrens.

Justice David had unmatched credentials for this case; however, this trial was to become one of extreme complexity framed around the relatively new scientific world of 'low copy number' (LCN) DNA technology.

Dieter Pfennig sat motionless in the courtroom, his face an unreadable mask. Dressed in a light blue prison tracksuit, he listened through headphones as the prosecution presented their case, betraying no emotion and barely acknowledging his surroundings. In stark contrast, Mr and Mrs Bell sat side by side in the public gallery, their hands tightly clasped together. Though their faces were marked with deep sorrow, there was a quiet strength in their unity. Their grief was palpable, yet they held each other up, drawing on a reserve of resilience that had spanned over three decades. They had come for one outcome—justice. The Bell family had endured an earlier trial (Geesing) that failed to bring them closure. Now, they listened once more as the state accused a man who had once been their neighbour, a man prosecutors said had stolen their child from the safety of her bed.

## Prosecutor Sandi McDonald

Fighting for justice for Louise was entrusted to one of South Australia's finest legal minds.

Anyone familiar with criminal trials in South Australia would instantly recognise Sandi McDonald, the state's most senior prosecutor.

Her story began far from Adelaide—in the grey, windswept city of Dundee, Scotland. Born into a family with dreams larger than the cold horizons of their homeland, Sandi was six years old when her parents, Eddie and Sandra, packed up their modest life in 1975. With little more than determination and hope, the McDonalds and their daughters, Sandi and Lisa, boarded a ship bound for a new life in Australia, part of the wave of migrants seeking opportunity in the 1960s and 70s.

Sandi thrived in her new home, excelling at school and eventually pursuing a law degree. While her peers chased clerkships with polished commercial firms and pictured careers in boardrooms, Sandi saw a different path.

Worried that she might miss out on job opportunities, she wrote a simple letter to then Attorney-General Chris Sumner. That letter landed on the desk of Paul Rofe QC, the formidable Director of Public Prosecutions, who offered her a temporary role. She thought it would be a brief stop. It wasn't.

From that humble beginning, Sandi McDonald rose steadily to become the longest-serving and most senior prosecutor in the Office of the Director of Public Prosecutions. Over nearly 30 years, she prosecuted hundreds of serious cases, many involving South Australia's most notorious criminals. Her name became synonymous with tenacity, precision, and the unwavering pursuit of justice.

Her experience and command of the courtroom were once again on full display in the trial for Louise.

From the moment McDonald opened the case, the prosecution's strength was clear: science. The verdict would hinge on how effectively the DNA evidence was explained to the jury. The rest of the case was circumstantial—some of it, admittedly, weak. But McDonald knew how to make evidence speak for itself.

**"A billion to one"**

Sandi McDonald didn't waste time giving the Adelaide media an eye-catching headline. She claimed DNA taken from Louise Bell's top showed that the possibility that anyone other than Dieter Pfennig abducted and murdered Louise Bell was "one billion to one". McDonald claimed the pyjama top of Louise's was ripped in such a way that it appeared as if someone had attempted to remove it, "particularly if her hands were bound".

McDonald revealed that a witness would give evidence that would match the German-born teacher's accent to that of a man who made a phone call to one of Louise's neighbours, claiming responsibility for the crime. She said they would also match Pfennig to a man who took a taxi driver on a "bizarre" drive-by of key locations in the case two months after Louise's disappearance.

McDonald said that Pfennig had also confessed to Bell's murder to two separate prison inmates. She claimed Pfennig had told one inmate he would not reveal where Louise's body was and claimed her death was an accident. He allegedly told the second inmate he saw no point in confessing, as "I know I'm not going to make it out of prison, why should I bother?"

The prosecution's strategy was clear: build the case layer by layer with circumstantial evidence, each piece adding weight until there was no room for reasonable doubt.

## Circumstantial Evidence — What is it?

The term 'circumstantial evidence' is regularly mentioned, but what exactly does it mean?

In 1866, English Judge C. B. Pollock described circumstantial evidence in a way that still resonates today.

"It is more like the case of a rope comprised of several cords. One strand of cord might be insufficient to sustain the weight, but three stranded together may be sufficient strength. Thus, it may be in circumstantial evidence—there may be a combination of circumstances, no one of which would raise a reasonable conviction, or more than a mere suspicion; but the whole taken together may create a conclusion of guilt with as much certainty as human affairs can require or admit of."

The case against Pfennig could be summarised with the following arguments:

1. Opportunity – Did Pfennig have the opportunity to commit the crime?
2. Proximity – Pfennig lived only 10 minutes away from the Bell family home.
3. Could it be proved that Pfennig had an obsession with the disappearance of Louise Bell?
4. Was the European accent of the caller to the Bells' neighbour on January 17, 1983, that of Dieter Pfennig?
5. Was there a connection between the Bell and the Pfennig

families? This would explain a scenario where Pfennig lured Louise Bell from her bedroom, as distinct from forcing her.

6. Were the conversations Pfennig had about the body of Louise Bell being in the Onkaparinga River, where he frequently canoed, proof that he was connected to the crime?
7. Was there forensic evidence connecting Louise's pyjama top, the Onkaparinga River and Pfennig's involvement in the same river?
8. DNA evidence linking Pfennig to Louise's pyjama top; was it 100% conclusive?
9. Pfennig's confessions to fellow prisoners that he murdered Louise Bell. Could the prisoners be trusted?

**Opportunity**

Pfennig was a keen canoeist, and so he and his family decided to attend a canoeing marathon over the 1982 Christmas/New Year period, which extended from Yarrawonga to Swan Hill in Victoria. Pfennig was a member of a support team for a competing canoeist. The Pfennig family set out on their trip early on Christmas morning in the family station wagon.

Witness, Reginald C, gave evidence that when the canoeing marathon finished on 31 December 1982 at Swan Hill, he returned to Adelaide with Pfennig as a passenger in his Kombi Van (towing a caravan), arriving back in Adelaide on the evening of 3 January 1983. Records show that Reginald C returned the caravan to the business from which he hired it on January 4, 1983. Pfennig's wife, Sandra and the children had driven the family car to Broken Hill to spend time with her mother and father. Dieter Pfennig was home alone on the night Louise Bell disappeared. The Pfennig family home was only a 10-minute walk from the Bell home.

## "There goes my alibi"

Witness RP, a neighbour of Pfennig, told the court that he was asked by Pfennig "to water the lawn and look after the place" while he and his family were away on the canoeing marathon. Pfennig informed RP that they would be "away for a couple of weeks."

RP described to the court the significant presence of police and searchers in Hackham West when it was discovered that Louise was missing. He recalled the occasion when the police door-knocked his street. RP was watering Pfennig's front lawn when an officer approached him. He told the officer that Pfennig and his family had gone away on holiday and informed the officer that Dieter Pfennig was a schoolteacher and a "respectable member of society."

Later that day, RP returned to Pfennig's home and was startled when he saw a curtain move in the lounge room. He knocked on the front door, and a dishevelled-looking Pfennig appeared. RP informed Pfennig about the police's door-to-door search regarding Louise's disappearance. Pfennig sucked deeply on a cigarette before replying. He then said with a smile, "There goes my alibi."

RP gave further evidence that at one stage, Pfennig spoke to him about disposing of a body in the Onkaparinga River. RP was vague about the context of that comment and the exact time it took place. He claimed Pfennig said: "If you were disposing of someone, you could weigh them down and throw them in the river and they would be virtually impossible to find."

In cross-examination, RP admitted that it could have been in the context of the Richard Kelvin case, but he could not remember. He also accepted that Pfennig's comment about an alibi was said in a joking manner.

A statement by RP was initially given to police in 1990 after the arrest of Pfennig for the murder of Michael Black, 7 years after the conversation.

**Night Moves**

Witness Robert T lived diagonally across the road from the Pfennigs' home. The chilling nature of Robert's testimony painted a haunting picture of Dieter Pfennig's late-night activities. He recalled seeing Dieter pacing the streets in the dead of night, his figure moving like a shadow under the streetlights.

"I couldn't see what he was doing apart from just walking up and down the streets," he said. "When I saw him outside our window, I would watch him to see what he was up to… he would eventually go away."

His observations, while mundane on the surface, carried an unsettling weight, considering the horrifying events that would unfold.

Sandra, Pfennig's ex-wife also shed light on her former husband's nocturnal habits. She claimed Dieter had struggled with insomnia for as long as she knew him, often walking or running the streets after dark to clear his mind. "He always said he had to get out," she recalled, offering a glimpse into his restless nature, one that echoed through the testimony of others who would soon be drawn into the trial.

But a casual conversation from nearly three decades earlier would later spark suspicions. A library assistant who worked with Pfennig at Mitchell Park High School recalled an unsettling remark he made in 1983. They had spoken about the disappearance of Louise Bell, and Pfennig had casually explained how a child could be abducted under the cover of night. Pfennig had told her, "I used to walk the streets to clear my head, and there was never anyone else around. It was possible to carry a child down the street without detection." The conversation was innocuous at the time, but it now seemed all too telling in hindsight. Yet, it wasn't until a 2011 newspaper article reignited memories that the library assistant would come forward, almost thirty years later.

\* \* \*

As the trial unfolded, the prosecution painted a grim picture of what may have transpired that fateful night. They argued that Louise Bell had not been forcibly snatched through her bedroom window as initially believed, but had been lured out, coaxed away by someone she trusted. Someone who had access to her life, her world. A person like Dieter Pfennig.

The revelation sent shockwaves through the courtroom, shattering the public's long-held belief that a stranger had committed the crime by reaching into Louise's room and lifting her out. To abduct a child from the safety of their bedroom required an intimate knowledge of the child's life and environment—something only a person close to Louise could possess.

Testimony from Petra Pfennig, Dieter's daughter, added a disturbing layer to the case. She remembered Louise from their shared school days, recalling how the two girls had played basketball together at Hackham West Primary School. "We were friends but not everyday playmates," she testified. "I remember a trip we took into town to watch adult players. Louise was with us, and we played punch buggy in the back of the bus." But Petra's memories went beyond school trips and childhood games. She also remembered a school camp with Louise in Mount Gambier, where the two girls had sat alone, a quiet isolation that would now seem deeply significant.

Yet, perhaps most unsettling were the inconsistencies Petra recalled in her father's stories about the night Louise disappeared. Dieter's explanations would change as the years went on, twisting and turning like a man who was losing his grip on reality—or perhaps hiding something darker. "I remember him saying he came home with us," Petra testified, "but I knew that wasn't right. Dad had a habit of changing the subject when I brought up things like this."

Even more chilling were her memories of a conversation with her father in the years following Louise's disappearance. Petra recalled Dieter mentioning Louise's younger sister, Rachel, in a conversation that now haunted her. "Dad said Rachel might be scared of being abducted, too," she recalled. "He said it might be because Louise was pretty, and Rachel was trying to make herself ugly so she wouldn't be taken, too."

Petra's testimony wasn't only about facts; it was a window into the mind of a family grappling with the horror of what might have been. Dieter Pfennig's daughter seemed to be the one person who might truly understand the contradictions in his words and the shifting nature of his memories.

## Petra, Louise, and Pfennig

One witness gave evidence via a video link from Queensland. She grew up living close to Pfennig's home and knew the Pfennig family well, as she also went to Hackham West Primary School and would walk to school. She told the Court that she saw Louise in Petra's company on approximately six different occasions. She said that on each occasion, they were heading away from Hackham West Primary School and walking towards South Road, up Glynville Drive. On the occasions she observed them, she said she was waiting for her girlfriend. On each occasion, Louise was walking with Petra, and Dieter Pfennig was there, and they were walking as a group. She particularly noticed Pfennig because he wore dark pink flared trousers. The sightings occurred over a short period, possibly spanning three to six months, with the last occasion at least a year before Louise was reported missing.

## Preoccupation with Louise

The prosecution presented numerous witnesses during the trial, with varying degrees of reliability. The Crown wanted to create a strong link between Pfennig and the Onkaparinga River because the person who planted her pyjama top on the lawn of the Hackham West resident had to be the killer of Louise Bell.

The prosecution believed that Pfennig had become preoccupied with Louise's disappearance. A variety of witnesses gave evidence of him making comments about her abduction while canoeing along the Onkaparinga River, and also when he was teaching in the classroom.

Mr KH was a Mitchell Park High School counsellor and became

friends with Pfennig. He kept in touch with Pfennig for several years after he was imprisoned for the Michael Black murder. He gave evidence that on one occasion in the staffroom, at about the time of Louise Bell's disappearance, Pfennig said that he was not allowed to discuss the matter because he was a person of interest. That was not the case at the time. Pfennig was only questioned about Louise after he was arrested for the murder of Michael Black.

In cross-examination, Mr KH agreed that he was first spoken to by the police about Pfennig in December 1990. Still, he said nothing about Louise Bell or Pfennig being a person of interest in relation to Louise Bell.

Another witness, a Mitchell Park High School teacher, testified that he was part of a car-pooling arrangement that included Pfennig from 1986 to 1988. At one point, Pfennig spoke about the Bell abduction and stated that he was able to assist the police because his daughter, Petra, and Louise were close friends who often had sleepovers at each other's houses. The witness also stated that Pfennig had once remarked, "It is surprising what you can see in windows when you go jogging at night."

The prosecution then called witnesses who testified about conversations with Pfennig regarding Louise while canoeing. Pfennig was an active member of the canoeing club and the South Coast Youth Club, where he went on to become a gym instructor. He was well-respected in the club and played a significant role in securing equipment for the club that was headed for the dump from local schools.

Neil C met Pfennig when he became involved in the South Coast Youth Club in the late 1980s. They would canoe together on most

Sundays in an area on the Onkaparinga River called Perry's Bend and sometimes further on to another spot called Shelly's Beach.

Neil C: He [Pfennig] was paddling along, and he mentioned that his paddle had tangled up in some bones he thought might have been human and told me that around the corner, the police found some pyjamas or substance, to do with Louise Bell.

Q. You said he told you he had come across these bones paddling, and then you said he probably thought they were human.

A. Yeah.

Q. Did he say that to you, or is that something you're assuming?

A. He told me, I think, yeah.

Q. You also said that he said something like there were traces or a substance on her pyjamas.

A. Yeah.

Q. Do you remember what word he actually used to describe what was on the pyjamas?

A. No, not really; not really.

Q. Did he say anything about where that trace or substance may be located?

A. Yeah, he told me that the police should be searching that area.

Q. For what?

A. For Louise Bell, they searched the area.

Q. I want to know whether your recollection of the conversation was to the effect that the police had searched the area and found something concerning Louise Bell's pyjamas, or that they should search the area. Do you remember what the conversation was?

A. They should search the area.
Q. Which area was he referring to?
A. Shelly's Beach.
Q. Where were you on the river at the time that was said?
A. In that area.
Q. When he said that to you — and you mightn't be able to tell us now, but tell us if you can—given you were in the area of Shelly's Beach, did he use the words 'Shelly's Beach' or some other words?
A. Shelly's Beach.

Another witness, Nicola D, disclosed that she would go canoeing with a group that included Pfennig. She recalled a conversation near the mouth side of Perry's Bend about the topic of missing children. She said that Pfennig became grumpy after that conversation and rowed to the other side of the river, got out of his canoe, and announced that he was going to walk back. She also gave evidence of another conversation at Neil C's house during which Pfennig told her that streetlights were turned off at 11.00 pm in his area until Louise Bell was found missing. He said that after that, they left them on all night.

The final witness on this topic was Mark F, who said that when he went canoeing with Pfennig, Pfennig would occasionally mention the name of Louise Bell. At one point, while canoeing together, Pfennig indicated an area of the river and said, "Louise Bell's body is here." He told the court how the conversation began:

Q. How did it come up?
A. We were just talking. I think it was a religious debate of some

sort, and as we were going further down the river, we spotted a dead sheep sitting or floating on the banks of the river, just on the water's edge.

Q. When you say 'we'...

A. Both Neil and myself, and I think what I recall is that Neil, to break the ice—he might have seen it was getting a bit heated at the time and he said, 'Look, there's a dead sheep', and he said, 'Dieter, have you seen any dead bodies in the river?', and he [Pfennig] turned and said 'Louise Bell's body is in there', and at the time we went past there was a lot of reed grasses and things like that.

Q. What was he pointing to?

A. He wasn't sort of pointing. He turned and nodded.

Q. What was he nodding to?

A. There was an area on the left side of us where there were reeds.

Q. Reeds.

A. Reeds, yes.

Q. And it was near the bank.

A. A bank, to the middle of that part of the river.

In cross-examination, he told police about the matter only days before the trial. He agreed with the defence counsel that the accused's comment could have been interpreted as a joke or a silly remark.

**European accent**

Ms S was always going to be a significant witness in the trial as she was the Hackham West resident who received the phone call from the abductor and also found Louise's pyjama top on her front lawn. In 1983, she lived with her two sons at Underbank Grove, Hackham West. Her estranged husband had left her in 1981. She knew the Bell family but was not familiar with Pfennig or his family. Underbank Road is connected to Meadow Way (the Bell family home) and is a short distance from Holly Rise (the Pfennig family home).

She repeated the evidence she gave thirty years previously at the trial against Raymond Geesing.

She told the court that on 17 January 1983, she received a telephone call from an unknown person. She was so alarmed by the call's initial contents that she took detailed notes and referred to them when giving evidence.

The male caller said he needed help, "that he was in a desperate situation and her help could save someone's life". She told him that he should not be ringing her but should be ringing the appropriate authorities. Reading from her notes, Ms S said that he replied that he could not ring any place where his voice could be traced and talked about tones and frequencies. She said he initially sounded upset because there was a quaver in his voice, and he appeared to need to take deep breaths, but after some time, he settled down.

He said that Louise Bell was with them, she was happy with them, and she did not want to go home. She questioned the caller to determine whether it was a genuine call, and he replied that to prove he had Louise Bell and that it was a genuine call, her earrings could be found if the police looked under a broken brick on the corner of South Road and Beach Road. During the call, he said that the South Australian Police were stupid and had missed several things. She described the voice as that of a male about 20-30 years old and thought she could detect a slight European accent. She said it was not English, French or Asian. It was broadly European, and she could not be more specific. He also sounded intelligent and was well-spoken.

Ms S then explained to the court that on the morning of February 28th, she noticed an item on her front lawn. She initially thought it was rubbish and ignored it. At that time, she was taking her son to school, and when she returned at about 9:00 am, the item was still in the same place, so she retrieved it. After a time, she realised that Louise Bell had been wearing a pyjama top when she disappeared and then phoned the police.

It is clear that the person who made the phone call was the abductor and murderer of Louise.

It must be recorded that Ms S gave evidence in the first murder trial that she believed the mystery caller's voice to be that of Raymond Geesing.

Another interesting fact that emerged was that Louise's earrings were found at the corner of South and Beach Roads, across from a building that had once been the Morphett Vale Primary School. After the school closed, the building was used as a library frequented by the Pfennig family, and later became a community centre where Dieter Pfennig played chess.

**Pyjama Top**

The court heard from several eminent scientific witnesses concerning the top. Authorities had performed a battery of tests on the top back in 1983/84. Foreign microscopic items were removed from the pyjama top and subjected to forensic testing. Material recovered from the pyjama top was consistent with having emerged in the Onkaparinga River, where Pfennig often used to canoe.

Testing also indicated that the pyjama top had been washed in household tap water at some point after being taken out of the river.

Taking the stand, Colin Bell's voice was steady, but the weight of three decades of grief pressed down on every word. He confirmed to the court what investigators had already determined—the pyjamas that yielded the crucial DNA match had belonged to his missing daughter, Louise.

He knew because the manufacturer's tag had been removed. It was a small detail that only a father would remember. Louise had asked for the tag to be cut off because the fabric was itchy. The pyjamas had been a Christmas gift.

It is worth noting that Colin Bell's evidence differed from that of his wife, Dianne, who did not give oral evidence in the trial. However, her evidence in the Geesing trial was tendered. She said that the pyjamas, and in particular the top, were passed on to Louise by her younger sister, Rachel, as they used to wear each other's clothes. She said that Rachel wore them a couple of times and Louise had them for a matter of months.

Mr Bell described Louise as a quiet, obedient child—gentle, bookish, and deeply fond of music. She was cautious around strangers.

He explained that the night she vanished, life in the Bell household had been routine, even joyful. The family had planned a simple weekend: shopping, a picnic, and a trip to see E.T., the movie every child talked about that summer.

But that night, small moments of sibling rivalry played out between Louise and her sister. They shared a bedroom, and Louise was excited about her new cassette recorder. She wanted to listen to music, but her sister did not. Mr Bell checked on them several times as they squabbled over the volume.

He was the last person to see Louise alive.

"She was still awake," he recalled. "But she didn't respond when I said goodnight to her."

Then, after a pause, his voice softened.

"It was my usual habit to kiss them goodnight," he said. "But I can't remember whether I did or not that night."

A father's last memory of his little girl—so ordinary, so fleeting—before she was gone forever.

### Returning to the scene of the crime

The prosecution presented a police statement taken on March 22, 1983, from a taxi driver, Richard Medlycott (deceased). In that statement, Medlycott said that he was working as a taxi driver in the city area at about 12.30 pm on Wednesday, 16 March 1983, near the junction of Bowden Street and Franklin Street. A man approached him and said he wanted to go to Hackham West. The passenger said he would tell Medlycott where he wanted to go when they arrived. Eventually, the man directed Medlycott to Meadow Way, which forms a junction with Glynville Drive. When they arrived, the passenger said, "Turn around and drive slowly back where you came." Medlycott did so and saw that the passenger was looking out of the window towards the houses on the western side of Meadow Way. The passenger then told him to stop. The passenger got out and walked down the length of Meadow Way. He paused for about two or three minutes and then walked back towards the car, while smoking several cigarettes. When Medlycott asked whether he was having difficulty finding his way, he was told to mind his own business. The mysterious passenger then directed Medlycott to stop outside Hackham West Primary School. He got out of the car again, looked around at the school while smoking, then walked back to the car and asked to return to the Franklin Street bus station.

Medlycott described the passenger as Australian in appearance, of medium build, with brown to dark hair of medium length and a receding hairline that extended back towards the temples, and clean-shaven, with a slight hint of whiskers. He wore thick-rimmed dark bifocal spectacles. He appeared to be in his late 30s or early 40s and was approximately 5'8" to 5'9" tall. He said he spoke with a slight European accent. He said the passenger smoked about 15 to 17 cigarettes during the time he was with him, and they were black, possibly with a different coloured tip.

Could it have been Pfennig in the taxi? Why would he go to the trouble of getting a taxi from the city when he lived close by? The description of his extreme smoking habit, his height, and age and European accent was certainly a close description of Pfennig. Was Pfennig playing out some sick fantasy?

The prosecution sought to argue that this was a further piece of circumstantial evidence that pointed towards Pfennig's preoccupation with Louise Bell's disappearance.

The taxi driver's evidence was so tenuous that its very inclusion raises questions about the judgement behind its presentation. An identification so uncertain that it is far more plausible that the person was a local or interstate investigative journalist, rather than the accused.

Moreover, a critical investigative step appears to have been overlooked: there is no indication that detectives verified whether Pfennig was in attendance at school on the day in question.

## "That guy's coming back"

As part of the circumstantial case, the court heard evidence from Ms B. She told the Court she would often visit her elder sister, who lived at Malpas Street, Old Noarlunga, in 1983. She could be certain of the dates because her niece, her sister's daughter, was born on 7 January 1983. Her sister's address was adjacent to a road that led down to the Onkaparinga River.

When her niece was about six weeks old, on what she believed was a Saturday, Ms B observed her sister standing at the kitchen window and calling out to her to look at this "guy".

Ms B looked out the window and saw a man walking towards the river. About half an hour later, her sister told her, "That guy's coming back."

Ms B said that her dog ran out, and this person stopped in front of the window, and they had a close view of him. He bent down and patted the dog, and Ms B noticed that he was completely wet, although fully clothed. She also noticed that he had something in his hands. She said it was a piece of clothing, but not a towel. The man then walked away from the river. She said his hair, although wet, was straggly, and she could not recall whether he had any facial hair.

Ms B said the man appeared to be in his mid-20s. She initially reported the incident in March 1983 and gave another statement in July 2012. On 14 July 2012, Ms B viewed a photographic identification pack prepared by Detective Campbell Hill. A photograph of Dieter Pfennig was included in the pack. Ms B was unable to make an identification.

When cross-examined, she agreed that when she spoke to the police in 1983, she did not mention that the man's clothes were wet; however, she maintains that the situation was unclear at the time, and the 1983 statement was not taken down accurately. She also agreed that in the 1983 statement, she never mentioned the man holding anything. Nevertheless, she was adamant that he was holding something that appeared to be a piece of clothing.

The prosecution sought to draw the inference that Pfennig was that man and on that date was retrieving the deceased's pyjama top from the Onkaparinga River.

Once again, this additional piece of circumstantial evidence stretched the prosecution's narrative to its limits. Why would Pfennig, who had access to a car, choose to walk to the river in full view of the neighbourhood? And if he intended to retrieve Louise's pyjama top, why would he do so at a time when he could easily be seen and identified? Furthermore, why would the prosecution draw the court's attention to the significant differences between Pfennig's appearance and Ms B's description of the man she saw?

**Little Louise**

For those who had followed this tragic case, it was a small comfort, perhaps even a relief, to hear Louise Bell remembered not only as a victim, but as the kind, gentle child she had been. The courtroom listened intently as Priscilla G, Louise's teacher in 1982, spoke of the little girl she had come to know so well.

"I got to know her very well," Ms G said, her voice steady but filled with emotion. "She was the type of child you only get every few years... she was quite unique."

She explained that Louise was different from most children her age. While her classmates ran outside to play at recess, Louise preferred to stay behind, helping her teacher in the quiet of the classroom.

"She didn't want to go out and play with the other children," Ms G said. "She was shy, quiet ... she just wanted to help. Every recess, every lunch, she wanted to stay."

Ms G would gently encourage her to go outside to spend time with her classmates. But Louise would always give the same answer: "I'm fine, I'm happy. I just want to stay and help you."

It became a familiar sight—Louise walking beside her teacher during yard duty, her small hand tucked into Ms G's. After school, she would linger in the classroom, tidying up, waiting for her parents to pick her up.

"She was so polite," she recalled. "She always wanted to please, always respected adults. She was just... lovely."

There was one time, however, that Louise had stepped out of her comfort zone. Much to Ms G's surprise, Louise had joined in a pillow fight with the other children during a school camp. She had also, unexpectedly, signed up for the school's basketball team.

The court heard that Patricia M coached that team. Ms M took the stand, providing further glimpses into Louise's quiet but sweet nature.

Both Louise and Petra Pfennig—the daughter of the accused—were on the team, though Petra was more of a reserve player and did not always attend games. Ms M recalled that she had occasionally driven Petra home but had little interaction with her parents, Dieter and Sandra Pfennig.

Asked about the girls' relationship, she said Louise and Petra "were really good friends."

"How do you know that?" the prosecutor asked.

Ms M smiled softly. "The normal little girl chitter-chatter," she said. "They would whisper and giggle together, the way young girls do."

Then, the courtroom watched something extraordinary—a moment frozen in time. A grainy home video, recorded during the basketball team's breakup barbecue in November 1982, flickered to life on the screen.

For a moment, Louise was there again.

In the footage, she is wearing bright yellow bathers, splashing in Ms M's pool, and laughing with the other girls. Later, after the pool party, she stands proudly as she receives a trophy. In the background, her father, Colin Bell, who had occasionally helped with the team, watches on.

Ms M recalled that Petra was also there that day. Her father, Dieter Pfennig, had picked her up from the party.

It was the last time she ever saw Louise.

## Pfennig's bizarre story

During proceedings, a 2011 video was played to the court showing Pfennig being questioned by major crime detectives regarding the disappearance and murder of Louise.

Pfennig told police he had no involvement in Louise's disappearance, then flatly denied his guilt in the murder of Michael Black. He told detectives he was "serving time for something I haven't done," insisting that his conviction showed how "things can get twisted around and misused."

The courtroom then listened in silence as a bizarre and unsettling piece of writing was introduced into evidence—a manuscript penned by Dieter Pfennig himself.

Titled "Faster Than the Speed of Thought", the story had been written in Pfennig's gaol cell before his arrest in November 2013. But it wasn't only a creative exercise. To detectives, it was something far more disturbing.

The manuscript told the story of two comatose children—orphans of different tragedies, a Japanese boy and an African girl, whom Pfennig called "The Golden Twins." Each had suffered unimaginable loss. The boy had survived an earthquake in Japan, while the girl had been left parentless by a brutal act of ethnic cleansing. Both ended up unconscious, taken to the same hospital in Beijing.

The story also featured a warrior—an ominous figure—who attempts to rescue the girl. But in the end, she refuses to go with him. She is killed.

The eerie themes did not go unnoticed by investigators.

But years later, when police seized Faster Than the Speed of Thought from his cell, Pfennig had one question for them.

"Do I get this all back?" he asked. "Some of it is work in progress."

It was an odd choice of words for a man accused of unspeakable crimes.

Detective Brevet Sergeant Anthony van der Stelt, of SA Police Major Crime, took the stand to describe what investigators had uncovered. He explained that the manuscript spanned multiple chapters, running to hundreds of pages.

"It starts off with an introduction," he told the court, "Essentially warning the reader not to read the book."

The second chapter was chillingly titled Violent Earthquake and Ethnic Hatred.

Detective van der Stelt described how the story opened in Japan, where a mother dies in an earthquake, leaving her young son critically injured and unconscious. He is taken to a hospital in China, where he remains in a coma indefinitely.

Then, the story shifts to Africa.

"There's a woman at home with her daughter," van der Stelt recounted. "There's an attack on this woman, and she is murdered. Her child is badly injured—again, unconscious—and is rescued by aid workers."

That girl, like the boy, is taken to the same hospital in Beijing.

And somewhere in this strange, dark tale was the figure of the warrior—the one who tried to take the girl. The one she refused. The one who killed her.

The prosecution let the details linger in the air.

## Enough Rope

The Adelaide Advertiser highlighted a haunting photograph from a Mitchell Park High School 1987 Year Book during the trial. The reporter gave a startling reveal:

"The teenage boy has been bound with a thick length of rope that loops over his neck, around his body several times and secures his hands in front of him. He looks at the camera over the top of a gag as an adult male leads him through the Upper Sturt scrub, half-smiling at the photographer.

It was meant to be a harmless, if somewhat tasteless, memento of Mitchell Park High School's 1987 "Rough It Camp," but the man holding the rope is a convicted child killer.

Dieter Pfennig posed for the disturbing photograph only two years before he murdered Michael Black and four years after he allegedly abducted and murdered Louise Bell."

## Chapter 3

# Prisoner Evidence

The announcement that the prosecution would call upon two long-serving prisoners to testify in the case of Louise Bell's murder sent ripples of unease through the courtroom. The twist in this tale was hard to ignore. It felt a little déjà vu.

Thirty years earlier, in a case that was both a tragedy and a miscarriage of justice, Raymond John Geesing had been convicted primarily on the testimony of prisoners, only to have his conviction overturned. The key witnesses—men with questionable motives and unreliable memories—had recanted their statements, leading to a stunning appeal win in 1985. Geesing's conviction was ultimately deemed a grave error. It was a case where the wrong man had been sent to prison, all because of a tangled web of lies spun by inmates. Now, with the trial of Dieter Pfennig, could history be poised to repeat itself?

One of those prisoners, a man known only as Prisoner X (PX), stepped into the witness box with a tale that seemed ripped from a twisted playbook of manipulation and self-preservation.

PX gave evidence about a damning conversation he allegedly had with Pfennig. PX, who had spent much of his life in prison, said that on or about Christmas Day, possibly in 2005, while he and Pfennig were smoking marijuana (yes, they were in prison!) Pfennig talked about the Michael Black case. PX recalled that Pfennig said he could not tell the authorities where the body of Michael Black was because Louise Bell, whom he described as "Bell", was also there. Pfennig then showed PX a street directory on his computer, indicating where the Bell family lived and where he had lived at Hackham West. According to PX, Pfennig said he took her and that there had been an accident. He also said that Louise went with him willingly. PX said that during this conversation, he and Pfennig were both affected by cannabis.

PX said that it was while he and Pfennig were both incarcerated in the Mount Gambier Prison that Pfennig made admissions to him about Louise Bell.

Q. When did the conversation occur?
A. Christmas.
Q. By that, do you mean Christmas time or Christmas Day?
A. Christmas Day.
Q. Why is it you remember that so clearly?
A. Because I gave Noel Thomas… when I went up to the canteen, he was waiting for a money order to clear or a cheque to clear, so I bought him a packet of White Ox and he says he'll pay back. Well, his family didn't come up and pay him, but he had some pot, so he gave the pot to me, and when he gave it to me, he said, 'Here then, have a merry Christmas.'
Q. And is that why you fix this as being Christmas?
A. No, because we were drinking bourbon that day. CT, an outside worker, had brought into the gaol, and there were a

few of us who were drinking that, and another prisoner had made up his own alcohol, and everyone was drinking that, so everyone was, yeah, a little bit drunk that day.

Prisoner X went on to explain how some of the prisoners had heard about how Pfennig could make his pet budgie defecate on command.

Q. How did it unfold from there? What happened from there?
A. I think it was AJ who said, 'Well, go show him,' and I followed Dieter into his room.
Q. What happened from there?
A. We went in. His budgie was in the room, and he was doing something or other and, sure enough, the bird shat on command.
A. After a little while, we had a few cones and I don't know, he was just looking at the computer really blank, and he started getting a little bit emotional, started sobbing a bit. I asked him what his problem was, and he said, 'Doesn't matter,' and I said, 'Well, hang about, we're having cones. What the fuck?', and he sort of just went weird and didn't say anything for a little while, and then said he couldn't say anything and—no, sorry, he was talking about Michael Black first, and he was saying about how what happened with Michael. I don't know why he brought that up.
Q. What was he saying about Michael Black?
A. How he had met Michael, and he had a conversation with

him, and Michael had left where he was up the riverbank, and he left a dog there.

Q. How did the conversation progress from there?

A. We had another cone and then I'd asked him—I assumed, because he had been sentenced for it, that they'd found Michael, and I asked him, 'Did they find him?', and there was just nothing, and then he said that he couldn't say anything, and I just left it at that for a little while, and then I asked him again and he said that there was—he couldn't say anything to anybody because there was somebody else there.

Q. What was said from there?

A. I really wasn't sure what he was talking about. I asked him what he was talking about, and he turned around and said that there was somebody else there. I again asked 'Who?', and he said that there was a chick there. I asked, 'Which chick?', and he said, 'Bell.'

Q. How did the conversation proceed from there?

PX went on to explain that Pfennig started to work on his computer. Pfennig then showed him a map of Hackham West on the screen.

A. He showed me a picture of where he lived and where Louise lived.

A. While he was still doing that, I was having a cone, and then he turned around and said, 'I did it.' I had no idea what he was talking about, and I asked him, and he said, 'I took her,' and I sort of said, 'Yeah, whatever.'

Q. Did you know what he was talking about at that stage?
A. Not really. The penny hadn't sort of dropped. I had had a cone.
Q. So, how did the conversation go from there?
A. He went on to say how they were together and how he knew Louise prior to what had happened, because I think I asked him, 'Why?', and he said that he knew Louise and Louise's family prior to what had happened from school.
Q. Did he say anything on the topic of how he killed her, how it came about?
A. No, just that it had been an accident.
Q. Did he explain how it had been an accident?
A. No. I didn't ask. I didn't know whether to believe him or whether it was just cones or—I didn't really know what it was.
Q. What happened from there?
A. And then I brought back up the subject of Bell... I just asked him something about Bell and he just went off topic, again, was talking about something else, and then we went back on to Bell and he explained how she was taken out from the window and as he was talking, he done like an L shape—it's your normal L, but he was facing me, so it was a reverse L.
Q. Did he say anything on the topic of how she got out of the window?
A. Willingly. She went with him willingly, and I didn't ask for any other reason. I wasn't really sure what to ask him or what to say, and then just out of the blue he said he took an item of clothing back, I don't know if it was inside the house to his

house, all I know, there was an item of clothing taken back to the house and he had neatly folded it. I asked him why he did that... he said because he felt guilty.

Prisoner X admitted that even though he and Pfennig were smoking a large quantity of cannabis (up to five cones), he believed he was not affected to any great extent; however, he believed Pfennig was much more affected and became emotional and cried while making the admissions.

Prisoner X spoke to the police about Pfennig's alleged confession on 9 October 2011 after his wife had read an article about the case in the Sunday Mail.

Grant Algie, QC, for Pfennig, cross-examined the former inmate about his criminal and medical history, claiming he told lies to be the centre of attention.

He suggested the former inmate's evidence was "a complete fabrication", to which the man replied: "f--k up, idiot, it's not."

"Whatever, homeboy — I think you're false, too," he said.

The former inmate emphatically refuted suggestions he wanted attention or to be in court.

"I f--king hate it, you're all a bunch of clowns in here," he said. "You're not my friends, I hope you all just f--k off."

Algie also tendered a statement from back in 1983 from police officer, Geoffrey Lancaster, who spoke of an incident involving Prisoner X. PX had attended the Port Adelaide police station and stated that a person had told him that they had abducted and murdered Louise Bell and also that the body of Louise Bell was in a quarry in the

Adelaide Hills. It appeared that PX had a long-held obsession with the disappearance of Louise. The likelihood of the judge accepting Prisoner X's evidence was diminishing. Still, it was about to take another hit when the defence called evidence from Dr Jules Begg, a practising psychiatrist with considerable experience with prisoners. He reviewed the medical records of PX and the statements that he made in relation to this matter. Begg claimed that PX suffered from an antisocial personality disorder, which exhibited certain narcissistic features. His opinion was that a person suffering from such a disorder can be unbelievable and untruthful.

**Stephen Akpata**

Stephen Akpata, aged 52, was born in Nigeria, where he became a Baptist minister. He arrived in Adelaide in February 1994 and soon found himself in trouble with the South Australian Police, primarily due to fraud and deception. In July 1996, he was sentenced to 12 months in prison. On 3 August 2001, he was further imprisoned for 12 months. On 30 May 2007, he was imprisoned for five years, with a non-parole period of three years, for various fraudulent offences. On one occasion, Akpata duped an Adelaide charity by promising to bring basketball legend Magic Johnson, as well as legendary boxers Evander Holyfield and Joe Frazier, to Adelaide for a Christmas charity event.

He liked to be referred to as 'Reverend' Akpata, author of the book Why Pray? He also defrauded the ANZ bank of $25,000 by writing cheques from his empty bank account. He also deceived WorkCover out of payments worth $17,000 by exaggerating a knife injury.

While in prison, he became friendly with Pfennig in his unofficial role as a prison pastor. He gave evidence that in late 2008, there was a conversation between himself and Pfennig at the Port Lincoln Prison in which Pfennig admitted that he killed Louise Bell. According to Akpata's testimony, Pfennig was remorseful and bearing his soul.

He and Pfennig were also together at the Mount Gambier Prison in 2008/09. Akpata ran a bible study group of which Pfennig was a member. During one of the meetings, notorious gunman Tony Grosser debated the subject of forgiveness and apologies to victims with Pfennig during a bible group meeting.

"Grosser made a grand statement that does he have to show remorse or apologise to SA Police who tried to shoot him and kill him," he said.

"Pfennig started on something and ended with something else… he contradicted himself… he argued for contrition and apologies to people, then against it.

"He's [Pfennig] an expert in every field, no matter what it is… he never keeps quiet; he's known for boasting."

Akpata said Pfennig approached him after the meeting to emphasise that he disagreed with Grosser, so the minister again encouraged him to confess.

"He said to me, 'It's okay for you… If you knew what I've done, you wouldn't say what you just said," he said.

"He said, 'Look at me, I've been here for nearly 20 years just for one offence — what do you think is going to happen to me about the rest?

"He said, 'I know I'm not going to get out of prison, why should I bother? Everyone has to deal with God themselves.'

"His tone was cocky, arrogant and self-defensive... quite the opposite of Mount Gambier."

Akpata said the last time the pair spoke was when he identified the manuscript as Pfennig's own story.

"From that moment, he never spoke to me about the book again," he said.

Akpata said he had neither asked for, received, nor been offered any benefit for giving evidence, nor expected one.

"Why would I?" he asked.

In cross-examination, Mr Algie questioned Akpata's honesty given his history of fraud.

Akpata objected to being asked questions about matters to which "I have pleaded guilty and made restitution."

"I'm not going to put my dignity down just because you are asking me questions," he said.

Mr Algie suggested Pfennig had never discussed Louise Bell with Akpata.

He further suggested that Pfennig's manuscript was actually about an African child and a Japanese child who communicated telepathically.

Akpata emphatically rejected those suggestions.

"I have no reason to come forward to give evidence and put myself through this trauma (apart from) my social and my conscience's obligations," he said.

The friendship between Pfennig and Akpata had developed to such a stage that on one occasion, there was a deep personal conversation between the two prisoners. He said that leading up to the conversation, it became apparent that Pfennig desperately wanted to speak to him about something that was troubling him. Akpata explained that the conversation occurred because of the arrival of a new inmate, Jamie Bell.

Q. So, where were you when this topic of Jamie Bell came up?

A. I recall him telling me, 'I hate the name Bell'... I recall him saying 'it's not the people, it's just the name Bell, that reminds me of the past, reminds me of a lot of things that I have eating at my heart and troubling me since I've been in prison'. And I said, 'If you have anything like that troubling you, talk to somebody about it, it's not about what you've done, talk to somebody about it,' and he said that is what he wanted to come and talk to me about, and then we scheduled another time for him to come and speak with me.

Q. Did he come and speak with you?

A. Yes, he did.

Q. Where did you speak with him the next time?

A. In my room.

Q. What was said on this occasion?

Pfennig told Akpata that when he was first imprisoned, he was loathed and hated for his murder of Michael Black, and at one time, a fellow inmate tried to kill him in the work gang in Yatala Prison.

Akpata described how Pfennig then began to get emotional.

"He began to shake, his whole body was shaking, and I told him, 'Calm down, you're already in gaol, this is not about what you are in gaol for?"

Pfennig: 'No, it is not about that, it is about what people don't know. That's why I hate the name Bell; there is a girl who died, Louise Bell.

I know everything about that girl. I carried her; I know where she is. I tried to calm her down, but she wouldn't cooperate'".

Akapta: And I think he said, "That is why or when I killed her."

Later that same day, Pfennig revisited Akpata.

Akpata: He asked me, 'Can God forgive someone who has done evil things like me? Because I've done things and I know things that are eating me up, and I do not want to go to my grave with them. And I said to him, according to the Word of God, that the only sin God cannot forgive is blasphemy against the Holy Spirit, the Son, or Jesus Christ.

Akpata urged Pfennig to tell the truth. Pfennig replied that he had already spent about 20 years in prison, and 'what do you think will happen to me? I know I'm not going to get out of prison. Why should I bother? What about the other ones?'

About four or five weeks before his release from prison in November 2011, Akpata saw a news item on television in which a detective was talking about a prisoner in the Port Lincoln Prison who had been questioned regarding the disappearance of Louise Bell.

After being released from prison, Akpata was placed in immigration detention awaiting deportation. In December 2011, he reported to the police his conversations with Pfennig. He gave evidence that he delayed telling the police because he did not trust the prison authorities and wanted to wait until he was discharged from prison.

In cross-examination, Akpata was informed that these conversations never occurred and that the details about the Louise Bell case were obtained from newspapers and television programs.

Akpata was also questioned on his motives, with Pfennig's defence revealing he had made a submission to the Federal Minister for

Immigration that he should not be deported because he was going to give evidence in this case. During an interview with an immigration official, Akpata also falsely claimed to be homosexual, such was his desperation to remain in Australia.[1]

---

[1] *Stephen Akpata was deported back to Nigeria and, in September 2017, was arrested for the murder of his newlywed wife. He was later found guilty and sentenced to death.

## Chapter 4

# Deathbed Confession?

The trial of Dieter Pfennig had already gripped the public with its dark echoes of the past. Still, no one could have predicted the extraordinary twist that unfolded on an otherwise unremarkable evening. On Monday, March 21, shortly before 7:30 pm, an emergency call pierced the routine at Yatala Labour Prison.

SA Ambulance Service paramedics rushed to the scene, finding Pfennig unresponsive, his heart having betrayed him in a massive cardiac arrest. By the time the paramedics arrived, Pfennig was clinically dead.

But death, it seemed, wasn't ready to claim him just yet.

Through swift intervention, the paramedics managed to revive him, snatching him back from the edge before racing him to the Royal Adelaide Hospital. There, he was placed in an induced coma, teetering between life and death, as doctors worked desperately to stabilise him. His condition was critical—his fragile heartbeat sustained only by machines and medical intervention. In the sterile, fluorescent glow of the ICU, Pfennig was no longer the cold, defiant figure seen in court. He was just another man clinging to life, his fate hanging by a thread.

Speculation in the media exploded almost instantly. Would the trial be abandoned? Had brain damage robbed Pfennig of the capacity to stand trial, offering him an escape from the justice he had long evaded? For the families of Louise Bell and other potential victims, the possibility was almost too much to bear. Michael O'Connell, a passionate spokesperson for Victims of Crime, voiced what many were thinking: "This is a genuine opportunity—should he recover—for him to let those people know where their loved ones are. So, they can pay the appropriate respect and bury them with dignity."

The idea of a deathbed confession hung in the air, heavy with hope. Would Pfennig finally unburden himself, revealing secrets he'd held close for decades? Or would he slip away, taking the truth to the grave?

Remarkably, Pfennig defied expectations once again—not only surviving, but recovering with a speed and resilience that astonished even his doctors. The man who had been declared clinically dead was soon described as alert, coherent, and—almost unnervingly—occupied with crosswords and sketching, as if the courtroom drama and his brush with death were nothing more than distant echoes. There were no signs of cognitive damage. No memory loss. No escape from justice.

Perhaps sensing an opportunity slipping away, his defence team pushed for additional medical tests, arguing that the trial should be delayed further. But the judge refused, unmoved by Pfennig's miraculous recovery or his lawyers' pleas. The trial would continue. Justice would not be postponed—not for four more weeks, not for a man who had already eluded it for far too long.

# Chapter 5

# DNA

During the trial, the court heard detailed evidence about the DNA analysis conducted on Louise Bell's pyjama top. In June 2011, South Australia Police (SAPOL) sent a petri dish and several tape lifts taken from the pyjama top to the Forensic Science Centre South Australia (FSSA). The amount of material available for DNA comparison was extremely small.

The petri dish contained vacuuming's collected in February 1983 from both the inside and outside surfaces of the pyjama top. After removing soil and other debris, forensic experts were left with a tiny piece of fluff. It was from this small fragment that they could extract DNA profiles. For comparison, DNA reference samples were obtained from members of Louise's family—Colin, Dianne, and Rachel Bell—as well as from the suspect, Dieter Pfennig.

When Pfennig was giving DNA to the authorities in 2011, he was in a jovial mood, telling them that his DNA "would be full of nicotine".

**The 17,000-to-1 Likelihood**

Initially, FSSA struggled to get precise DNA results. They then sent the samples to the Netherlands Forensic Institute (NFI), which specialises in analysing extremely small amounts of DNA using a method called "low copy number" (LCN) analysis.

Meanwhile, FSSA began using a new DNA analysis technique called STRmix. This method calculates the likelihood ratio, which helps determine the likelihood that a specific person contributed to a DNA sample. In August and November 2011, FSSA extracted DNA from the tape lift and the fluff using automated processes. To assess the results, they compared the DNA to databases from Caucasian and Bavarian (German) populations, given Pfennig's German background.

Using STRmix, FSSA concluded that the DNA profile found on the fluff was approximately 17,000 times more likely to have come from Dieter Pfennig than from an unknown, unrelated individual. This number represents the likelihood ratio, a statistical measure indicating strong support for Pfennig being a contributor to the DNA.

**The NFI Analysis**

The courtroom fell silent as the prosecution revealed a powerful new player in the case against Dieter Pfennig: the Netherlands Forensic Institute.

This wasn't just any lab. It was the same world-renowned facility that had helped identify nearly every victim of Malaysia Airlines Flight MH17, a plane torn from the sky over Ukraine. Now, it was their work that stood at the centre of the charges against Pfennig.

Justice Michael David listened intently as prosecutors explained that the NFI had uncovered DNA evidence linking Pfennig to the disappearance of young Louise. The match was no coincidence, they argued—it was scientifically airtight, with a margin of error so small it defied imagination: one in a billion.

The court was told this wasn't the first time the NFI had taken on a case of international significance. War crimes tribunals in The Hague had sought their forensic expertise. They had traced DNA across decades, solved mysteries buried for generations, and built a national database so detailed it had identified century-old remains in long-forgotten cases.

Now, their work had led to the courtroom where Dieter Pfennig stood on trial—not only for a crime but also for a truth buried for years.

One of NFI's top forensic experts, Bart Jan Blankers, explained how his team specialises in Low-Template DNA analysis. The same technique allegedly ties Pfennig to Louise's murder.

"Low-Template DNA analysis is used when we have extremely small or degraded samples," he told the court. "It allows us to extract genetic information from evidence that, years ago, would have been considered unusable."

That technology, the prosecutors argued, is what finally cracked the case, decades after Louise vanished.

In early 2012, NFI received the DNA extracts from the tape lift and another from a stain on the pyjama top. However, the stain sample yielded no usable DNA results in Australia or the Netherlands. NFI also received reference samples from the Bell family and Dieter Pfennig. Later, in February 2015, they obtained a reference sample from Dieter's brother, Roland Pfennig.

The first step in NFI's analysis was to measure the quantity of DNA available. Due to the limited amount remaining, NFI scientists decided to rely on the DNA extraction results previously obtained by FSSA.

NFI expert Mr Blankers analysed the DNA from the fluff and found that it contained a mixture of at least two people, possibly three. There was no clear indication of a single dominant contributor, making it unsuitable for certain types of interpretation known as consensus methodology.

NFI then compared the DNA profile from the tape lift with reference samples from Colin Bell, Dianne Bell, Rachel Bell, Roland Pfennig, and Dieter Pfennig. All individuals, except Dieter Pfennig, were excluded as contributors to the major DNA profile.

To determine the statistical significance of the match, NFI calculated the random match probability using a Dutch Caucasian population database. This probability represents the likelihood that a random person from this population would have the same DNA profile. The result was astonishing: the chance of finding someone in the Dutch Caucasian population with a matching DNA profile was one in 5.766 billion.

In simpler terms, the evidence suggested that, based on the available data and statistical models, it was extremely unlikely that the DNA found on Louise's pyjama top belonged to anyone other than Dieter Pfennig.

## A Solid Defence

Submissions were made on Pfennig's behalf by two experienced counsel, Mr Grant Algie and Mr Paul Charman. Charman dealt exclusively with the DNA aspect of the case. He proposed that the DNA evidence amounted to the resolution of two questions:

1. Whose DNA is on the pyjama top?
2. If it is proved that it is Pfennig's DNA, how did it get there?

Paul Charman stood before the court, his arguments measured, his tone deliberate. His task was to plant a seed of doubt in the judge's mind, to unravel the certainty the prosecution sought to establish with forensic science.

Charman focused sharply on a critical point: the forensic analysis. He argued that the seemingly more sensitive system at the National Forensic Institute (NFI) failed to obtain a result from the fibre, commonly referred to as "the fluff." This failure, he contended, fundamentally undermined the credibility of the Forensic Science South Australia (FSSA) results, which had used a less sensitive system known as STRmix to produce a result. To Charman, it was incongruous—illogical, even—that a less sensitive system could succeed where a more advanced one had not. This discrepancy, he asserted, was a compelling reason for the judge to exclude the DNA weighting of 17,000:1 provided by FSSA, arguing it could not be considered proved beyond a reasonable doubt.

But Charman's defence did not rest solely on the technicalities of forensic science. He pursued a more profound question: was there an innocent pathway through which Dieter Pfennig's DNA could have been transferred into the Bell household?

Charman pointed to the undeniable connection between Pfennig's daughter, Petra, and Louise Bell. The two girls were not strangers; they played on the same basketball team, trained together weekly, and attended the same school. Their interaction was regular, sustained, and undisputed. Charman suggested that Pfennig could have come into incidental contact with Louise during these routine activities, perhaps while picking up Petra from school or attending a basketball game. This everyday contact, he argued, provided a plausible route for the transfer of DNA.

He proposed a chain of events grounded in the ordinary: Pfennig's DNA could have transferred to Petra through casual, innocent contact. From Petra, it might have passed to Louise through a shared basketball, a friendly hug, or any of the countless small interactions children have. Louise, in turn, could have carried this trace DNA into her home environment, which eventually settled on her pyjama top. Charman emphasised that before the judge could rely on the DNA weighting as circumstantial evidence, he must be convinced beyond a reasonable doubt that such a sequence of events could not have occurred.

In his closing address, Charman distilled his argument with clarity.

"We say the inconsistencies in the results cause there to be a lack of clarity about the strength of the DNA evidence," he stated plainly.

He outlined the two fundamental questions the prosecution needed to answer: First, whose DNA was found on the pyjama top? And second, how did it get there? Charman acknowledged that while the prosecution had presented extensive evidence addressing the first question, they had offered little concerning the second.

"The DNA evidence can never actually prove whose it is with absolute certainty—it's always a likelihood ratio," Charman reminded the court. "And how the DNA was transferred onto Louise's pyjama top cannot be known beyond a reasonable doubt."

He highlighted the regular, close contact between Petra and Louise at school, during basketball games, and at a pool party.

"At any one of those times, material and cells could transfer, and there's nothing to exclude that as a possibility," Charman argued.

Finally, he drew attention to the limited scope of the forensic evidence. The case, he said, hinged on two "tiny" DNA samples. No additional DNA evidence was found on Louise's bedroom window or elsewhere in her room.

Charman's meticulous arguments were designed not to deny the presence of DNA but to cast doubt on its origin and relevance. In the sterile language of forensic science, he found a narrative of uncertainty, one he hoped would resonate with the judge's sense of reasonable doubt.

## Beyond Reasonable Doubt

Paul Algie was no stranger to high-profile cases in South Australia. His reputation preceded him, having defended Bradley Murdoch in the infamous case of the missing English backpacker, Peter Falconio. Despite Algie's efforts, Murdoch was found guilty of murder. Algie had even drawn the ire of then-Premier Mike Rann, who publicly dismissed him as a "mullet-wearing lawyer" after a controversial trial verdict. Yet, in courtrooms, Algie was known not for his hairstyle but for his sharp, meticulous legal mind.

In this trial, Algie centred his argument on the crux of the matter: Had it been proved beyond a reasonable doubt that Pfennig was guilty? He likened the case to one of Australia's most notorious miscarriages of justice, stating, "This is probably South Australia's Azaria Chamberlain, where the public was shocked and outraged but also intrigued and drawn into the speculation of how this could have happened."

Algie approached the prosecution's case like a surgeon with a scalpel, methodically dismantling each piece of evidence presented against his client.

**Onkaparinga River Connection** — Algie conceded that Pfennig had ties to the Onkaparinga River through his involvement with the canoeing club. However, he quickly pointed out that countless others shared that same connection. "There were many people in the area, likely from even farther afield, who had similar associations with the river," he argued, suggesting that Pfennig's link to the location was hardly unique.

**Prison Informants** — Turning to the testimony of Prisoner X and Stephen Akpata, Algie urged the court to treat their words with caution. He reminded the judge that another man, Raymond Geesing, had been wrongfully convicted of this exact crime back in 1983, based heavily on the dubious evidence of prison informants. "History has shown us how unreliable such witnesses can be," he warned.

**Fading Memories** — Algie scrutinised the reliability of witnesses recalling conversations from three decades earlier. "Trying to remember a conversation from 30 years ago is almost impossible," he asserted. He highlighted that some witnesses only came forward in 2011, others in 2015, and one even after the trial had begun. "This isn't about their honesty," Algie clarified, "but about the natural erosion of memory over time."

**"There Goes My Alibi"** — Algie seized on one of the prosecution's key points: Pfennig's remark to his neighbour, RP, "There goes my alibi." Far from being incriminating, Algie argued it was the opposite. "Is that really what a guilty man would say to his next-door neighbour?" he asked, noting that RP himself admitted Pfennig had said it jokingly.

Moreover, RP's account described Pfennig as calm and unperturbed even after police visits, behaviour inconsistent with that of a guilty man.

**No Vehicle, No Crime?** — Another cornerstone of Algie's defence was the absence of a vehicle. At the time of Louise Bell's disappearance, Pfennig had no car. The family's only vehicle was with his wife, Sandra, who was visiting her parents in Broken Hill. "The abductor must have had a car," Algie insisted. "It's impossible to believe that a 10-year-old could have been taken without one, nor could a body have been transported to the Onkaparinga River without the use of a vehicle."

**The Wet-Clothed Man** — Algie pointed to the testimony of Ms Brannigan, who described seeing a man near the river in March 1983. Her description painted a picture of someone around 5'6", in his mid-20s, with straggly hair and no facial hair. "Compare that to Pfennig's appearance at the time: 6'1", 35 years old, with a distinctive moustache," Algie urged, referencing photos from a canoe marathon to support his argument. "The description simply doesn't match."

**The Taxi Driver's Statement**—Addressing the testimony of taxi driver Mr Medlycott, Algie questioned its credibility. "Why would Pfennig, if he wanted to revisit the crime scene, take a taxi from the city when he could have just walked from his home?" he asked. Additionally, Medlycott described his passenger as clean-shaven and around 5'8"—again, inconsistent with Pfennig's appearance at the time.

The Shadow of Raymond Geesing — In closing, Algie introduced a final element of doubt: the spectre of Raymond Geesing. "Although Geesing was acquitted by the Court of Criminal Appeal, that does not exclude the reasonable possibility that he committed the crime," he argued. For Algie, the question was straightforward: Was there room for doubt? If so, that doubt was reasonable, and his client deserved the benefit of it.

**Killer Taunted Police**

Sandi McDonald stood before the court, her voice steady, every word carefully chosen to thread together the complex strands of the Crown's case. She believed they had a critical piece of evidence—a definitive DNA link to Dieter Pfennig. But McDonald knew that DNA alone might not carry the full weight needed for a conviction. What would matter was the story woven through decades of Pfennig's actions—a trail he had left, perhaps unwittingly, from the moment Louise Bell vanished.

"All of these pieces together, layer upon layer, led to the person who had taken her—and that person, of course, we say, is Dieter Pfennig," McDonald told the court, her gaze unwavering.

She conceded there were mysteries still unsolved. How had Pfennig managed to abduct Louise without waking her sister or disturbing her parents? McDonald's theory was as chilling as it was plausible. "Even a strong man like the accused was then, to get into that room and get that child out physically without waking the sister up... the far more likely scenario is she was enticed out," she explained.

The audacity of the crime was staggering. "To take a child in the first place with the parents only metres away, to taunt the police through a third-party phone call, to lay a trail of her belongings—it's all incredibly audacious," McDonald emphasised, painting Pfennig not only as a predator but as someone who revelled in the risk, in the control.

She detailed Pfennig's peculiar behaviour in the years following

Louise's disappearance. He had often discussed the case with an intensity that raised suspicions. "He clearly wanted to talk about Louise Bell," McDonald said. "There was an unusual interest, almost as if he were re-living it, talking it up."

Then came the revelation that echoed through the silent courtroom. Pfennig had allegedly confided in a colleague that he was a suspect, long before he was officially identified as such. McDonald's voice sharpened with incredulity. "Why on earth would a father, teacher, a family man, be telling his colleague and friend that he was a suspect in the abduction and murder of a little girl when he's not?" she posed to the jury. "It makes no sense unless he's getting some sort of perverse pleasure, drawing attention to himself, continuing to talk about it."

She paused, letting the weight of her words settle.

"Thirty years later, the DNA profile from the pyjama top matches the accused. It matches the DNA of a man who was telling a colleague in a staffroom that he was a suspect."

The courtroom remained still, the echoes of McDonald's final statement hanging like an invisible thread, tying together years of silence, speculation, and now—evidence.

## Chapter 6

# Judgement day

The courtroom was packed—standing room only. Media crews jostled for position, detectives who had worked the Bell abduction for decades exchanged solemn nods, and Louise Bell's family sat clutching one another's hands. After thirty years, would justice finally be delivered to her grieving parents?

Justice Michael David took his seat, his presence commanding immediate silence. He methodically dissected the testimony that had been presented before him, dismissing the accounts of certain witnesses. Prisoner X and Stephen Akpata, he ruled, were unreliable. The testimony of taxi driver Mr Medlycott was deemed "too vague," while Ms B's account was described as "fraught with risk."

However, the weight of forensic evidence told a different story. Justice David ruled that the findings of both the National Forensic Institute and Forensic Science SA had been proved beyond a reasonable doubt.

"I accept each witness's evidence as a piece of circumstantial evidence to be regarded within the balance of the circumstantial case," he stated. "They do not, in isolation, amount to evidence of guilt beyond a reasonable doubt. However, the cumulative effect of each witness's evidence carries great force when assessed together, contributing to a full picture. Each piece is consistent and resonant with the others, forming a story of the accused's interest and involvement in the disappearance of the deceased."

Then came the defining moment.

"The accused's preoccupation with the deceased, and in particular, his references to the Onkaparinga River, is given great weight by the scientific evidence. That evidence definitively states that Louise Bell's pyjama top was submerged in that river. The area of submersion was one with which the accused was extremely familiar."

Justice David's voice remained steady as he delivered the words so many had waited decades to hear.

"I find that a combination of the above circumstances amounts to proof beyond reasonable doubt that the accused abducted and murdered the deceased."

The courtroom held its breath.

"I find the evidence of the DNA comparisons compelling. The fact that the pyjama top was washed in tap water before being deposited on Ms S's lawn leads me to a clear inference—there would have been more DNA present before that washing. When combined with all the other circumstances—the accused's connection to the Onkaparinga River, the comparison of accents with the voice of the person who telephoned Ms S, and the accused's opportunity, being alone in his house on the night of the abduction—I can see no other explanation to account for these proven facts other than his guilt."

Yet, even in his certainty, Justice David acknowledged lingering mysteries.

"I cannot say for certain how Louise Bell was taken from her room.

However, I find it difficult to believe that force was used. I think it more likely that the accused, to some extent, knew the deceased through his daughter and induced her out through the window. However, my inability to resolve that question does not affect my decision or cast any doubts in my mind about the guilt of the accused."

He continued; his voice heavy with the weight of the moment.

"I do not know how he actually killed the deceased, where he killed her, or where he put her body. These questions may never be answered. But they do not impinge upon the certainty of my verdict."

As the final words left his lips, Louise's parents embraced. Generations of police officers who had carried the burden of this case exhaled; their relief palpable. Acting Justice David then turned to an "unusual" matter, addressing defence barrister Grant Algie, QC, before sentencing submissions began.

"During this period of time, I say to your client—through you—if he could tell the authorities where the bodies of Michael Black and Louise Bell are, that may or may not affect his sentencing. I do not know," he said. "But I want to bring this whole ghastly thing to an end."

Outside the courtroom, a major crime detective read Colin and Dianne Bell's prepared statement to the media. Their words were filled with gratitude and a plea that had never wavered.

"Our beloved ten-year-old daughter was taken from her own bedroom—a place she should have been safe—and she has never come home. Words cannot describe the impact this has had on our lives. Today is the culmination of our struggles to find answers for Louise. This is what makes today's decision so important.

"We would like to thank everyone for their persistence and efforts in trying to return Louise to us and for prosecuting this matter. In particular, the police, the prosecution team, and the judge knowing it would have been an extremely difficult case to try.

"While today is a significant milestone, we want our daughter back. So, I appeal to anyone with information that might assist us in finding Louise to come forward now. While this afternoon's outcome is significant, it is only part of this terrible event. We still want to be able to lay Louise to rest."

Colin Bell looked on as police confirmed that neither they nor the family considered the case closed.

Detectives made their stance clear. Their goal from day one had been to return Louise to her family. Decades might have passed, but they would never stop searching until that promise was fulfilled.

## And in the End..

The nightmare that began on a warm summer night in 1983 has finally reached its grim conclusion over forty years after the heartbreaking disappearance of Louise. A guilty verdict has sealed Dieter Pfennig's fate—convicted of the abduction and murder of 10-year-old Louise Bell, the child who vanished from her bedroom in the dead of night, never to be seen alive again. Her death has haunted South Australia ever since, a cruel echo of innocence stolen.

Pfennig, already serving life for the murder of young Michael Black, will now die behind bars, caged like the depraved predator he is, deprived of the freedom he so violently stole from others. The State will feed him, clothe him, and provide him the mercy he refused his victims. This is justice by modern standards—merciful, humane, and restrained. But for those who loved Louise and Michael, true justice remains elusive, tangled up in the twisted mind of a man who will carry his truths to the grave.

Yet even in his imprisonment, Pfennig wields a final, cutting cruelty. He clings to his secrets, denying the grieving families the dignity of a proper farewell. No graves to visit, no bodies to mourn. Just unanswered prayers.

The damage he has caused is irreversible. The pain, the suffering, the grief—these will never fade. Police authorities on numerous occasions have pleaded with him to reveal the resting place of these two children, but Pfennig offers nothing.

Louise Bell was a shy, obedient little girl. As her father described, she was a child eager to please, the kind of girl who might have blended into any crowd, a lover of music, dance, and basketball. Her life was tragically snatched away by evil, leaving behind only the memories of what might have been.

Michael was a boy who seemed destined to follow in his father's footsteps. The great outdoors was his playground. Fishing, bird watching, and exploring nature were his passions—simple pleasures that should have filled his days with happiness and freedom. Instead, his life was also taken in an act of unspeakable cruelty.

The families of Louise and Michael were shattered, their lives permanently scarred by an unimaginable trauma. Decades later, the weight of their loss remains beyond measure. Yet the question lingers—were these children Pfennig's only victims?

## Did He Do Them All?

Dieter Pfennig was a master manipulator, skilfully hiding his violent fantasies behind the facade of an intelligent, family-oriented man. Those I've spoken to about Pfennig described him as "charismatic," "charming," "good-looking," "brilliant," though also "a bit strange," "controlling," "arrogant," and "moody." However, people who encountered Pfennig as a teacher glimpsed more of his true nature. One former police officer who had been one of his students recalled that during the summer, Pfennig often wore loose, baggy shorts without underwear, and at times, when he sat down, his genitals would be exposed. Another former student described how Pfennig would sometimes treat the senior students as if they were still in primary school. "He was a creep", according to one former student.

Was he born with evil embedded in his soul? Or did it emerge over time, shaped by his early life experiences? No one can say for sure. But I ask you, the reader, to consider this: Could Dieter Pfennig be responsible for murders other than Michael and Louise? Could he have been involved in some of the most bizarre child abductions in Australian criminal history?

The disappearances of the three Beaumont children and the abductions of Joanne Ratcliffe and Kirste Gordon are among the most chilling and mysterious cases in the world. Let me briefly remind you of these horrors.

On January 26, 1966, three children—Jane (9), Arnna (7), and Grant (4)—vanished without a trace from Glenelg Beach, Adelaide, never to be seen again. Despite numerous police investigations and years of speculation, no one has ever been able to identify a credible suspect in this case. Then, on August 25, 1973, two young girls, Joanne Ratcliffe (11) and Kirste Gordon (4), were abducted from the Adelaide Oval in broad daylight, amid thousands of spectators at a football match. Once again, the police could not name a viable suspect, and hardly anyone was ever seriously considered a person of interest.

So why would I draw a connection between Dieter Pfennig and these infamous child abductions? It is merely speculation, but I feel it is a question worth asking.

## January 1966

At the time of the Beaumont children's disappearance in 1966, Pfennig would have been only 18 years old. Was he too young to commit such an unthinkable crime? Experts in this field say he was of sufficient age. Studies of child killers reveal that the urge to kill can appear much earlier than we might imagine.

The psychology of serial killers—whether targeting children or adults—share certain disturbing traits. A child's fantasies, often born from abuse or neglect, can manifest in horrific ways. When raised in an environment where violence is common, a child may begin to fantasise about escaping to a world where they dominate others. These fantasies, once formed, can evolve into an insatiable need to act on them. For some, murder becomes a cyclical process, driven by the emotional gratification of repeating the crime.

Criminal psychologists note that serial killers—whether they begin their killing spree in childhood or adulthood—are marked by an absence of the fear of death. They derive pleasure from the act itself. They do not feel what most of us would call remorse, guilt, or fear—instead, the thrill of killing overrides any other emotion.

But what if Dieter Pfennig's fantasies turned to actions as a young man? What if he was responsible for the abductions of the Beaumont children and others? There is no solid evidence to prove this, but the patterns of behaviour exhibited by child serial killers and adult serial killers alike make the speculation all the more chilling.

Only time will tell if the true scope of his depravity will ever be fully understood. But for now, one issue is clear: Dieter Pfennig's reign of terror has ended, but the scars he has left on the hearts of the families affected by his crimes will never fade.

**Boyfriend**

During the early stages of the Beaumont investigation, detectives sought to gather information about the friends of the three children, particularly the eldest, Jane. The grieving mother of the children, Nancy Beaumont, had repeated her story to detectives so many times that the phrases felt brittle, splintered by grief and exhaustion. But a memory had surfaced that made the investigators sit up and take notice.

It was Arnna, her sweet, chatty seven-year-old, who had first mentioned it. That childlike candour—so endearing, so disarming—had made Nancy smile at the time.

"Jane's got a boyfriend down at the beach," Arnna had declared one afternoon, her tone light with the certainty only a child could possess.

Nancy had laughed it off. "Boyfriend" was simply a word to describe a new friend, a playmate picked from the sea of tanned and freckled children running wild through the sand and surf. It meant nothing. Or so Nancy had assured herself.

But now, seated in the suffocating sterility of the police station, the details felt barbed. Her stomach twisted as she recounted it to the detectives, their pens scratching feverishly against notepads. What was a moment of innocent amusement now felt like something more sinister.

My memory of Glenelg Beach in January 1966 is of a child's paradise — and a parent's uneasy dream. I was nine years old, on holiday with my parents and five siblings, the day the Beaumont children disappeared. My father remembered the beach teeming with families, all seeking relief in the cool ocean breeze. Trying to keep track of six children among hundreds—perhaps thousands—of beachgoers was overwhelming. At one point that afternoon, one of them vanished from sight. Panic surged through my father. He sprinted to the water's edge and spotted the missing child, drifting about two hundred metres offshore on an inflatable ring. Without hesitation, he plunged into the surf and swam out to bring my sibling safely back.

Beyond the sand, Glenelg Beach featured a summer carnival close to the foreshore. The carnival rides creaked and whirred — chipped horses bobbing on tired carousels, a Ferris wheel groaning as it turned. The men who ran them lurked in the shadows of their booths, faces hidden by sweat-stained caps, their cigarettes glowing like tiny warnings in the dusk. At times, they watched the crowds too closely, their gazes lingering too long.

Children darted between the rides, the girls in their bright summer dresses — lemon yellow, sky blue, cherry red — flashing like little beacons among the throng. Boys in their shorts and t-shirts ran amok with their water pistols. Mothers called after them, half-laughing, half-worried, their voices quickly swallowed by the clang of bells and the screech of rusted gears. Beneath the surface of the carnival's cheerful chaos, something darker seemed to pulse — unnoticed, but waiting.

Children and young adults lined up eagerly for the rough-and-ready dodgem cars or the thrill of the Big Dipper. Men showed off their skills at shooting bobbing ducks with well-worn slug guns. Sticks of fairy floss were everywhere, and the scent of freshly made doughnuts drifted enticingly through the air. Young couples strolled hand-in-hand along the crowded sideshow alley, weaving through the lively crowd. It felt like a place where innocence was untouchable.

But paradise had its shadows.

Was an eighteen-year-old Dieter Pfennig roaming around Glenelg Beach on January 26, 1966? Pfennig and his family had come to Australia from a fractured, weary Germany. They'd lived first at the Woodside Immigration Centre, tucked away in the calm seclusion of the Adelaide Hills. After three weeks, the Pfennigs were relocated to the beachside suburb. Glenelg became Dieter's escape and playground.

Glenelg's vibrant chaos, sunshine, and sea must have seemed like another world—dazzling and intoxicating for a boy raised amid the grey bleakness of post-war Europe. He would wander the beachside playgrounds with the hungry curiosity of someone determined to understand this new land.

Could Dieter Pfennig, with his youthful face and unassuming demeanour, have approached Jane, Arnna, and Grant Beaumont on that crowded beach? And more chillingly, could he have persuaded them to follow him away from the safety of the crowds? Was Dieter Pfennig Jane's so-called boyfriend?

Back in 2015, while researching my book, *The Missing Beaumont Children: 50 Years of Mystery and Misery*, I traced the paths Jane, Arnna, and Grant might have taken if they missed their bus and set out to walk home. From Glenelg Beach to their home on Harding Street, Somerton Park was a mere 2.5 kilometres. For the children familiar with the route, it was a straightforward, if wearying, 40-minute trek. But under the merciless January sun, with temperatures scorching Adelaide at 38.8°C, even a short walk could feel endless.

Jane and Arnna had proved their endurance only weeks before, strolling the length of Jetty Road from the picture theatre after watching *The Sound of Music*. But on January 26, 1966, with their four-year-old brother Grant in tow, their pace would have been slower. They'd have been more vulnerable.

One possible route passed near a property owned by a relative of Dieter Pfennig. It's speculation, indeed — but speculation grounded in the grim logic of abduction. To seize three children in broad daylight would have required several things: a vehicle, a secluded spot, and, perhaps most chilling of all, a plan.

Pfennig was just another young face in the crowd flocking to Glenelg Beach that sweltering day. But already, dark fantasies festered within him, cruelty waiting to be unleashed. Years later, his monstrous capacity for violence would be proved beyond doubt. But then, he was only a teenager, blending in with the heat-struck throngs.

Could he have lured them away with the promise of cool shade, a drink of water, a place to rest? Jane, saddled with the responsibility of her younger siblings, battled the relentless sun. Did a seemingly kind voice offer relief?

Pfennig held a driver's licence. Whether he had access to a vehicle remains uncertain. But to abduct three children under so many watchful eyes required either meticulous planning or the swift exploitation of opportunity. How could anyone, let alone a boy of eighteen, devise such a crime?

The question has endured, a sinister echo across the decades. Could a teenager, drawn to the beach like so many others, have committed one of the most bewildering child abductions in history?

And if he did, why did no one see it happen?

## August 25, 1973

At 10:30 am, Les and Kath Ratcliffe, along with their two children, Joanne (11) and David, headed towards the Adelaide Oval, six kilometres from their Campbelltown home. They were looking forward to watching a winter Saturday tradition: a football game between North Adelaide and Norwood.

Kirste Gordon (4) was at the game in the care of her maternal grandmother while her parents, Greg and Christine Gordon, were visiting friends with their younger daughter in Renmark. The two families were seated together in the Sir Edwin Smith Stand.

Ratcliffe's parents and Gordon's grandmother, who were friends, allowed the two girls to go to the toilet together on two occasions that day. The Ratcliffe family rule was that children were not allowed to go to the toilet during the breaks in the game or during the last quarter. The girls left to go to the toilet at around 3:45 pm. The Ratcliffe's began searching from around 4:00. After an unsuccessful first attempt, Kathleen Ratcliffe finally got an announcement on the oval's PA system shortly after the game ended around 5:00 pm. The girls were reported missing to the police at 5:12 pm.

The girls were never seen again.

## Adelaide High School

In the same year that Kirste and Joanne went missing, Dieter Pfennig (25) taught at the Adelaide High School situated in the parklands along West Terrace (2 kilometres from Adelaide Oval). He taught Science and Technology. Another science teacher at this school was Greg Gordon, the father of Kirste!

I have checked the records at Adelaide High School, and it has been recorded that Pfennig left the school in 1973. It is unknown on what date he left, or whether he left of his own accord, or for other reasons.

What a peculiar circumstance – a future convicted child abductor/murderer teaching with the father of a child that was abducted and murdered.

At the time, Pfennig, his wife, and their newly arrived daughter, Petra, lived on Henley Beach Road, Underdale, close to Kirste's grandmother.

## Peculiar calls

Pfennig revelled in the power of games. In the Louise Bell case, his cruelty was methodical and strategic. He phoned a neighbour of the Bells with a chilling, calculated hint: Louise was injured. He planted her earrings under a brick, hoping the police would find them, as if toying with them. He laid her pyjama top neatly on his neighbour's front yard, a grotesque mockery of innocence. Pfennig believed his intellect to be superior, his cunning unmatched. He dared the police to catch him, all the while maintaining his veil of innocence.

The neighbour described the caller's voice as having a subtle European accent. She was right.

During Pfennig's trial for the murder of Michael Black, another victim, this one who had survived, took the stand. Thirteen at the time the boy was abducted, raped and assaulted by Pfennig in 1990 at Port Noarlunga. He recounted their chilling conversations. At one point, Pfennig asked about the boy's father and whether he could afford to pay a $40,000 ransom.

For years, I dismissed the ransom talk as another mind

game—Pfennig's way of exerting control over a terrified child. But the mention of ransom stirred a dark memory from the Beaumont case.

In February 1966, only weeks after the Beaumont children vanished, *The News* reported a startling call. A man claiming to be holding the children for ransom phoned the newspaper; his voice was described as thick with a foreign accent.

"I want reward money for them. It will have to be a good reward."

He spoke to a telephonist but hung up before being connected to the editorial department.

The following day, Max Beaumont—Grant Beaumont's younger brother—sat anxiously in the editorial office of *The News*, waiting for the mysterious caller to try again. Max was desperate. As an interstate tourist bus driver, he had heard the shocking news of his brother's missing children over the radio while shepherding tourists through Tasmania.

Max pleaded publicly, his voice raw with anguish: "I have a special message from Grant and Nancy Beaumont. If the caller is genuine, I'll come to any agreement he wants to get the children back." His desperation was palpable. "I don't know where it will come from, but I'll raise it somehow."

But the call never came.

And yet, the ransom pattern didn't stop there. Years later, Kirste Gordon's father picked up his phone to hear a slow, deep voice deliver an ultimatum.

"I have your daughter."

"What…"

"$25,000."

The voice, thick with a heavy Australian drawl, was cold and mechanical. Mr Gordon demanded proof. The man's response was curt and chilling. "Never mind the proof. If you want to see your daughter alive, I want $25,000 by Thursday."

Then, silence.

The caller struck again at 6:50 pm, his voice the same slow, deliberate drawl. Mrs Gordon, trembling with rage and desperation, pleaded into the receiver, "If you have our daughter, let me hear her."

Click.

The phone went dead.

The police dismissed the caller as a hoax. But was it? Or was it something far more insidious? A twisted echo of the power Pfennig craved?

Pfennig had already proved his taste for psychological torment, planting evidence and luring police down false trails. He toyed with the families' hopes and fears, delighting in the confusion he sowed. Could he have been behind the calls to *The News*? A cruel, manipulative ruse to feel powerful?

And what about Kirste Gordon's father? Had Pfennig contacted him, with his voice altered to avoid recognition? Or was it someone inspired by his methods, feeding off the pain and anguish of others like some parasitic imitator?

Perhaps the calls were genuine attempts at extortion. But there's a darker possibility that fits all too well with Pfennig's sadistic gamesmanship: He never wanted money. He only wanted control. The power to manipulate. To torment. To force the families to dance to his sick tune. A way to assert dominance. To keep them guessing. To bask in their suffering.

And if it was Pfennig, his games were far from over.

## My theory blown apart..

I have to admit, there's a major flaw in my theory. The notion that Dieter Pfennig is the most likely abductor and killer of the Beaumont children, Kirste Gordon, and Joanne Ratcliffe has always seemed a cruelly logical fit.

The FBI, during a 2005 symposium in San Antonio, Texas, officially defined serial killing as "the unlawful killing of two or more victims by the same offender(s), in separate events." Others stretch that minimum to three victims, requiring a cooling-off period between murders and a passage of at least 30 days. By those definitions, Pfennig qualifies as a serial killer of children—a predator with a twisted mind and a calculated approach.

What are the odds of having more than one like him in a city the size of Adelaide? A city with a population of roughly 1.5 million. It seemed statistically improbable. Stranger murders are rare—stranger child murders are rarer still. The abductions of Louise Bell, Michael Black, Kirste Gordon, Joanne Ratcliffe, and possibly the Beaumont children felt like pieces of the same monstrous puzzle.

But the disappearance of Rhianna Barreau shattered that comforting sense of coherence.

On the morning of Wednesday, October 7, 1992, twelve-year-old Rhianna Barreau vanished from her home on Wakefield Avenue, Morphett Vale—only six kilometres from where Louise Bell had been abducted: a close radius, a cruel proximity. But Pfennig was in prison at the time.

It was school holidays, and Rhianna was eager to send a Christmas card to her overseas pen pal. She intended to catch a bus for the errand. But fate interfered. A sudden public transport strike thwarted her plans, leaving her to walk.

Rhianna's mother, Paula, left for work at 8:30 am. That morning, Rhianna was seen walking to the Southgate Square Shopping Centre at 10:30 am, where she purchased a Christmas card at 11:19 am. By early afternoon, she was seen crossing the grounds of Morphett Vale High School and Stanvac Primary School, a small bag in her hand, likely containing the card she'd bought.

At 12:30 pm, she was spotted walking along Highway Drive.

Police believe she made it home. The small bag containing the card was found untouched on the dining table. The television blared its lonely noise, and a vinyl record lay discarded on the living room floor. The house was locked.

However, when Paula returned home around 4:10 pm., her daughter was no longer there.

Two days later, the case was declared a major crime. The house Rhianna had returned to for safety had failed her. Whoever took her had come and gone without leaving a single trace. And they have kept their secret for over three decades.

Rhianna was never found.

Pfennig may have been the monster lurking behind so many unsolved disappearances, but Rhianna's abduction is proof he was not alone. There was another predator; another cold mind willing to seize a child in broad daylight and leave a family shattered.

The realisation gnaws at my theory like rust. Pfennig's guilt may be beyond doubt in the cases of Louise Bell and Michael Black. Still, the existence of another killer—a phantom who preyed on Rhianna Barreau—forces a reconsideration of everything.

South Australia harboured more than one predator willing to abduct and kill a child. This predator probably still shops amongst us all, walks the same paths, and still hides the darkest secret of all.

**September 1985**

While researching this book, I uncovered a fragment of information that had haunted the edges of my mind for more than a decade. It was buried in the September 1985 edition of the South Australian Government Gazette. I had expected nothing more than the usual bureaucratic clutter—builder's licences, council by-laws, the dull hum of officialdom. The gazette also listed crimes in South Australia. And then, in the middle of that monotony, it appeared.

*Pfennig, Dieter. Rape,*
*unlawful intercourse and sexual assault.*
*On bail.*

It was a bare-bones entry, stripped of context or explanation. But the name froze me. Pfennig.

I knew nothing about this charge—no details, no court record I could find. Surely, I thought, it couldn't be tied to the time Pfennig was caught 'fondling' a young chess partner, or to the boy who accused him of sexual assault during a fishing trip. Both of those incidents had evaporated without reaching a courtroom—mysteries in themselves. Was it simply the era? How did Pfennig commit crimes against children without going to court?

Weeks before this book was set to go to press, the answer began to take shape—purely by accident.

I had been chatting idly to a man I'd just met, my usual curiosity coaxing his story from him. I asked where he lived.

"Hackham West," he said.

When I told him I was writing about the abduction of Louise Bell, his entire expression changed—eyes narrowing, voice sharpening with something between memory and contempt.

"I used to live on Holly Rise," he said, "when Dieter Pfennig lived there."

What he told me next would finally shine light on that long-forgotten Gazette entry—and cast an even darker shadow over the murderous child killer. The following was a conversation I had with the former neighbour of Dieter Pfennig.

"I understand you lived on Holly Rise when Dieter Pfennig was there?"

Neighbour: "Yeah. I did. Back in the eighties. I'll never forget it."

"What was he like as a neighbour?"

Neighbour: "Strange. That's the first word that comes to mind. His eyes… they were just wrong somehow. Cold. He was furious with me once because I wanted to put up a high front fence. He said it would 'interfere with the walking path.' Truth was, my mate had seen him with binoculars, looking straight into my daughter's front bedroom. I wasn't having that."

"Did he mix much with people in the street?"

Neighbour: "He'd offer to 'tutor' the kids, one-on-one. Always seemed to find excuses to be around them. During school holidays, I'd hear his car heading out in the middle of the night. Two, three in the morning sometimes."

"There was an entry in the September 1985 Government Gazette – 'Pfennig, was charged with rape, unlawful intercourse, sexual assault.' Do you know what that was about?"

Neighbour: "I do. That was the neighbour's four-year-old boy. Pfennig sexually assaulted him in the shed next door. The boy's mother caught Pfennig in the act. Walked in on it. She was the only witness, but she couldn't testify—she had a complete breakdown. Ended up in psychiatric care. The case fell apart on the day of the trial."

"You've mentioned his car going out late at night."

Neighbour: "Always. Especially during the holidays. I'd be lying in bed, hear the engine turn over, and watch him drive off into the dark. I reckon a lot happened in those hours nobody ever knew about."

The neighbour's recollections were not just unsettling—they were a map of warning signs that went unheeded. A man watching children's bedrooms through binoculars. Offering one-on-one "tutoring" to the young. Slipping into the night in his car while the rest of Hackham West slept.

Looking back, that 1985 charge feels like a fork in the road—a moment where the course of lives could have been altered. A guilty verdict then would have ended his freedom, cut short the nights of prowling, and locked the door on future victims. One in particular stands out like a shadow on the page: Michael Black.

If justice had been served in 1985, Michael might never have crossed Pfennig's path. He might be alive today.

## Sandra Pfennig: A Life Overshadowed

The heartache of the parents of murdered children can never be fully comprehended. The despair they must feel and carry forever is something akin to living in hell. But they are not the only ones to suffer at the hands of murderers like Pfennig.

Sandra Pfennig was born and raised in Broken Hill, a rugged, isolated town in the heart of the Australian outback. Broken Hill is renowned for its rich mining history, particularly for the world's richest deposits of silver, lead, and zinc, as well as its strong union movement. Broken Hill shaped Sandra with a sense of resilience and independence that would serve her well in the years to come.

In 1968, at the age of 18, Sandra left Broken Hill for Adelaide to study primary school teaching at Bedford Park Teachers College, which was then shared with the newly established Flinders University. It was an exciting time, full of promise and possibility.

It was at college that she met Dieter Pfennig, a fellow education student training to be a high school teacher. Sandra remembers him vividly: "He was charming, charismatic, good-looking. He had so many interests—he could talk about anything." But while he seemed intelligent and engaging, Dieter wasn't a dedicated student. He failed his first year and often spent long hours indoors. Concerned, Sandra encouraged him to take up canoeing, hoping it might help.

Dieter rode a BMW motorcycle at the time, but Sandra disliked being a pillion passenger. So, she bought her own: a brand-new Yamaha 250cc speedster. It wasn't just a practical move—it sparked a lifelong passion for motorcycling and long-distance travel, including a solo journey to North Queensland and international adventures to places on every continent of the world.

In 1972, Sandra and Dieter married. They lived in a modest two-bedroom unit. The following year, their first daughter, Petra, was born. In 1977, they purchased a home in Hackham West and settled into what appeared to be an ordinary suburban life.

On December 30, 1989, Sandra received a call from Christies Beach Police Station. It was Dieter. He'd been arrested for the kidnapping of a young boy from Port Noarlunga and wanted a solicitor. At the time, Sandra was running a local community legal service. Disgusted, she left a message for a solicitor and walked away. She had a holiday to Vanuatu planned in two days and refused to let Pfennig's chaos interrupt her life again.

She had found freedom leaving Pfennig. Unbeknownst to Dieter, his arrest marked the beginning of the end. His freedom was gone forever.

When questioned by police, Sandra described Dieter as a chameleon: "He could be a perfectly competent teacher, a kind friend, a loving father. He played the roles well. But he was a sociopath—always lying, always manipulating. He knew exactly what he was doing."

As Pfennig's crimes became public—first the Port Noarlunga abduction, then his link to the 1989 murder of Michael Black—the emotional weight intensified. Pfennig's parents had the gall to blame

Sandra. "If he had never married you, none of this would've happened," they told her.

"His father was strict and domineering," Sandra said. "There was a lot of control in that household. But blaming me? That was their way of avoiding the truth."

Rather than return to public life, Sandra chose to focus on her children and her well-being. She earned degrees in Psychology and Legal Studies and began to rebuild her life quietly.

**Petra**

Researching for books like this is a slow, grinding process. You spend years chasing fragments of truth, reaching out to people scarred by crime or entwined in its shadow. But amid all that darkness, you meet remarkable souls—people whose resilience somehow burns brighter because of what they've endured.

Petra Pfennig was one of those people.

I first contacted Petra in 2014. Our conversations played out over the phone, filtered through email exchanges. I expected anger or defensiveness—anything but the calm, measured strength she displayed. It wasn't defiance or denial—it was something more complex. She had a strong moral code.

Petra described her father as a "good dad."

It struck me like a stinging slap in the face. How could a man like Dieter Pfennig, who is responsible for so much pain and suffering, ever be considered "good" by anyone? But the more I delved into how killers live double lives, the more I began to understand.

Men like Pfennig compartmentalise. They neutralise guilt and keep their worlds separated—one life for their families, their friends, the innocents they would never dream of harming. Another life for their prey. Strangers who mean nothing to them, disposable victims whose suffering is merely a consequence of their twisted desires.

Petra grew up believing her father was innocent. His guilt, when it finally became undeniable, shattered her. She had to reconstruct her understanding of the man who raised her—a man who played the role of a loving father even as he preyed on children.

By the time I contacted Petra, she had already begun the brutal work of rebuilding her life. She approached me with empathy and kindness despite the monstrous truth she carried like a scar. It wasn't only her pain she acknowledged—it was the pain of her father's victims, their families, the countless lives torn apart by his crimes.

I made a mistake.

I sent Petra a manuscript draft detailing some of the most graphic moments of Pfennig's sadism—the account of the boy who escaped from him. I had thought she might offer insight, a fresh perspective. Instead, I reopened wounds that had barely begun to heal.

Petra replied with a message revealing the depth of her suffering and resilience. "I need to keep positive thoughts and let all the awful stuff go," she wrote.

And then, something that took me by surprise. "Remember that I send a prayer every day to the children involved. I will never give up trying to get my dad to be honest with himself. Maybe one day we will know where the bodies are."

Those words lingered. A child of a killer, praying every day for his victims and fighting, in her own quiet way, for justice and truth.

Petra had long since accepted the horror of her father's crimes, but she hadn't surrendered to despair. Instead, she channelled her grief into empathy and action. Where others might have turned their backs, Petra reached out—both to the victims her father had wronged and to her father himself, demanding the truth he still refuses to give.

Courageously, Petra gave evidence in her father's trial because she believed in revealing the truth. She did it for Louise and Michael.

She was his daughter. She had every reason to deny what he was. But she didn't.

Petra's courage in the face of a reality most of us could never fathom left me with an admiration I wasn't expecting. Not everyone touched by evil lets it consume them. Some fight against it, even when their blood carries the stain.

After reading her message, I wondered if Pfennig truly understood what he had lost—a daughter who still wanted answers but who had also moved beyond him, a daughter stronger than he could have imagined.

## About the Author

**Michael Madigan** is an Australian author who writes compelling true crime and investigative works that delve into some of the nation's most disturbing and unsolved mysteries. His titles include *The Missing Beaumont Children – 50 Years of Mystery and Misery* and *The NCA Bombing: A Mafia Murder*. Crimes that have haunted Australia for decades.

Michael's writing is driven by a deep sense of justice and a fascination with the human stories behind criminal cases—his style is meticulous, compassionate, and unflinching.

In addition to his true crime works, Michael co-wrote *Bush Legends* with his brother Anthony, celebrating uniquely humorous Australian football yarns, and co-authored *Red Tape Rape: The Life of Ki Meekins*, the remarkable true story of Ki Meekins' fight for justice after surviving child sexual abuse and taking on the South Australian Government in court.

When not researching or writing, Michael bushwalks, reads true crime, and explores Australia's enduring mysteries. He is currently working on his next true crime book.

**Other titles by Michael Madigan**

*The Missing Beaumont Children:
50 Years of Mystery and Misery*

*A Mafia Murder? the NCA Bombing*

www.ingramcontent.com/pod-product-compliance
Lightning Source LLC
Chambersburg PA
CBHW020752160426
43192CB00006B/310